CAKES
biscuits&slices

THE AUSTRALIAN
Women's Weekly

Of all the things I really love to cook, I think that baking a cake or a few dozen sweet biscuits must rank at the top of my favourites list. It's as much of an emotional reward (treating and pleasing my family and friends) as it is a physical one – witnessing how the combination of a few simple ingredients like flour, butter and sugar somehow wondrously come together in an almost heaven-sent result.

Pamela Clark

Food Director

contents

CAKES

The cake you make yourself, whether a special occasion crowd-pleaser or a simple family favourite, is a sure-fire way of letting family and friends know you care. And, since skill is less of an issue than is an attitude of steady-as-she-goes, baking any cake in this chapter will be as easy for the beginner as for the expert. Whichever recipe you decide to make, read it straight through before getting out the cake pans: that way there'll be no unhappy surprises and so you'll be able to give full attention to following the recipe step by step.

If you can't find pecan meal, simply blend or process 150g of roasted pecans until they are finely ground. Be sure to use the pulse button, however, because you want to achieve a flour-like texture, not a paste.

chocolate and pecan torte

PREPARATION TIME **20 MINUTES** COOKING TIME **1 HOUR (PLUS STANDING AND REFRIGERATION TIME)**

200g dark eating chocolate,
  chopped coarsely
150g butter, chopped
5 eggs, separated
¾ cup (165g) caster sugar
1½ cups (150g) pecan meal

GANACHE
½ cup (125ml) cream
200g dark eating chocolate,
  chopped coarsely

1. Preheat oven to moderate (180°C/160°C fan-forced). Grease deep 22cm-round cake pan; line base and side with baking paper.

2. Stir chocolate and butter in small saucepan over low heat until smooth; cool 10 minutes.

3. Beat egg yolks and sugar in small bowl with electric mixer until thick and creamy. Transfer to large bowl; fold in chocolate mixture and pecan meal.

4. Beat egg whites in small bowl with electric mixer until soft peaks form; fold into chocolate mixture, in two batches. Pour mixture into pan; bake about 55 minutes. Stand cake 15 minutes; turn, top-side up, onto baking-paper-covered wire rack to cool.

5. Meanwhile, make ganache by bringing cream to a boil in small saucepan. Remove from heat; add chocolate, stir until smooth.

6. Pour ganache over cake; refrigerate cake 30 minutes before serving.

Before grating the lime, make sure it is at room temperature and roll it, pressing down hard with your hand, on the kitchen bench. This will help extract as much juice as possible from the fruit. You can substitute the same weight of other citrus fruit – lemons mandarins, blood oranges, oranges, etc – for the limes if you wish.

lime and poppy seed syrup cake

PREPARATION TIME **20 MINUTES** COOKING TIME **1 HOUR**

¼ cup (40g) poppy seeds
½ cup (125ml) milk
250g butter, softened
1 tablespoon finely grated lime rind
1¼ cups (275g) caster sugar
4 eggs
2¼ cups (335g) self-raising flour
¾ cup (110g) plain flour
1 cup (240g) sour cream

LIME SYRUP
½ cup (125ml) lime juice
1 cup (250ml) water
1 cup (220g) caster sugar

1. Preheat oven to moderate (180°C/160°C fan-forced). Grease base and sides of deep 23cm-square cake pan.
2. Combine poppy seeds and milk in small jug; soak 10 minutes.
3. Beat butter, rind and sugar in small bowl with electric mixer until light and fluffy. Add eggs, one at a time, beating until combined between additions; transfer mixture to large bowl. Stir in sifted flours, cream and poppy seed mixture, in two batches.
4. Spread mixture into pan; bake about 1 hour.
5. Meanwhile, combine ingredients for lime syrup in small saucepan. Stir over heat, without boiling, until sugar dissolves. Simmer, uncovered, without stirring, 5 minutes.
6. Stand cake 5 minutes, turn onto wire rack over tray. Pour hot lime syrup over hot cake.

Unless a recipe instructs you to do otherwise, use roasted unsalted nuts when making a cake since the butter you use has probably already had salt added to it. Buy the freshest nuts you can: they should taste slightly sweet. And be sure to taste any nuts you've had around for a while before using them to make certain they haven't gone rancid.

pistachio buttercake with orange honey syrup

PREPARATION TIME **20 MINUTES**   COOKING TIME **50 MINUTES**

2 cups (280g) unsalted pistachios,
    chopped coarsely
185g butter, softened
1 tablespoon finely grated orange rind
¾ cup (165g) caster sugar
3 eggs
¼ cup (60ml) buttermilk
1½ cups (225g) self-raising flour
¾ cup (110g) plain flour

ORANGE HONEY SYRUP
1 cup (220g) caster sugar
1 cup (250ml) water
1 tablespoon honey
1 cinnamon stick
1 teaspoon cardamom seeds
3 star anise
3 strips orange rind

1. Make orange honey syrup; cool.
2. Preheat oven to moderate (180°C/160°C fan-forced). Grease 23cm-square slab cake pan; line base and sides with baking paper, extending paper 2cm over the sides. Sprinkle nuts evenly over base of pan.
3. Beat butter, rind and sugar in small bowl with electric mixer until light and fluffy. Add eggs, one at a time, beating until just combined between additions; transfer mixture to large bowl. Stir in combined buttermilk and ⅓ cup of the orange honey syrup, and sifted flours, in two batches.
4. Spread mixture into pan; bake about 40 minutes. Stand cake 5 minutes; turn, top-side up, onto baking-paper-covered wire rack. Brush surface of hot cake with half of the remaining heated syrup.
5. Cut cake into squares, serve warm, drizzled with remaining heated syrup.

ORANGE HONEY SYRUP Stir ingredients in small saucepan over low heat, without boiling, until sugar dissolves; bring to a boil. Remove from heat; cool 15 minutes then strain.

Raisins and other dried fruits are generally "plumped" to rehydrate them before being stirred into a cake mixture and baked, otherwise, the fruit is likely to remain as it is, dry, chewy and tough, rather than melt-in-your-mouth luscious. Any raisins that have clumped will also separate in the boiling water. Craisins, dried sweetened cranberries, can be rehydrated exactly as the raisins are, and used instead, in this recipe.

boiled raisin chocolate cake

PREPARATION TIME **20 MINUTES** COOKING TIME **1 HOUR 20 MINUTES (PLUS COOLING AND STANDING TIME)**

2 cups (300g) raisins
2 cups (500ml) water
1 teaspoon bicarbonate of soda
⅓ cup (35g) cocoa powder
2 teaspoons ground cinnamon
½ teaspoon ground clove
1 teaspoon vanilla extract
250g butter, chopped

1½ cups (330g) caster sugar
4 eggs
1½ cups (225g) plain flour
1 cup (150g) self-raising flour

CHOCOLATE GLAZE
200g dark eating chocolate,
  chopped coarsely
100g butter, chopped

1. Preheat oven to moderate (180°C/160°C fan-forced). Grease 24cm bundt pan well.
2. Combine raisins and the water in medium saucepan; bring to a boil. Reduce heat; simmer, uncovered, 10 minutes. Remove from heat; stir in soda, cocoa, spices and extract. Cool to room temperature.
3. Beat butter and sugar in medium bowl with electric mixer until light and fluffy. Add eggs, one at a time, beating until just combined between additions; stir in combined sifted flours and raisin mixture, in two batches.
4. Spread mixture into pan; bake about 1 hour 10 minutes. Stand cake 5 minutes; turn onto wire rack to cool.
5. Stir ingredients for chocolate glaze in medium heatproof bowl over medium saucepan of simmering water until smooth. Pour glaze over cooled cake; stand 30 minutes before serving.

Frozen blackberries are sold in most supermarkets in 300g packages – and since our cream filling only calls for half that amount, thaw the remainder and serve them with the roulade. When folding the dry ingredients into the creamy egg and sugar mixture, use a large metal spoon, rubber spatula or whisk. You can also use your hand like a rake. Wheaten cornflour results in a slightly better sponge than does maize cornflour (milled from corn). This sponge can also be made in a 22cm-round cake pan, greased with butter and floured lightly, and baked in a moderate oven (180°C/160°C fan-forced) about 20 minutes. Turn sponge, top-side up, onto a baking-paper-covered wire rack. Split the sponge in half and join the halves with berry cream.

berry cream roulade

PREPARATION TIME **15 MINUTES** COOKING TIME **12 MINUTES**

3 eggs
½ cup (110g) caster sugar
½ cup (75g) wheaten cornflour
1 tablespoon custard powder
1 teaspoon cream of tartar
½ teaspoon bicarbonate of soda
1 tablespoon caster sugar, extra
1 tablespoon icing sugar

BERRY CREAM
¾ cup (180ml) thickened cream
1 teaspoon vanilla extract
1 tablespoon icing sugar
1 cup (150g) frozen blackberries,
  chopped coarsely

1. Preheat oven to moderate (180°C/ 160°C fan-forced). Grease 25cm x 30cm swiss roll pan; line base and two long sides with baking paper, extending paper 5cm over long sides.
2. Beat eggs and caster sugar in small bowl with electric mixer about 5 minutes or until sugar is dissolved and mixture is thick and creamy; transfer to large bowl.
3. Sift cornflour, custard powder, cream of tartar and soda together twice onto paper then sift over egg mixture; gently fold dry ingredients into egg mixture. Spread sponge mixture into pan; bake about 12 minutes.
4. Meanwhile, place a piece of baking paper cut the same size as swiss roll pan on bench; sprinkle evenly with extra caster sugar.
5. Turn sponge onto sugared paper; peel away lining paper. Use serrated knife to cut away crisp edges from all sides of sponge, cover sponge with a tea towel; cool.
6. Meanwhile, make berry cream; spread cream over sponge. Using paper as a guide, roll sponge gently from long side to enclose filling. Dust with sifted icing sugar.

BERRY CREAM Beat cream, extract and icing sugar in small bowl with electric mixer until soft peaks form; fold in thawed berries.

A passionfruit is well-named: the fruit's simultaneously sweet and tart taste inspires an almost addictive passion in the person savouring its seedy, yellow pulp. Its singular flavour marries well with yogurt and creamy desserts like panna cotta, ice-cream or bavarois. You will require about seven passionfruits for this recipe.

passionfruit and lemon syrup cake

PREPARATION TIME **20 MINUTES** COOKING TIME **1 HOUR**

⅔ cup (160ml) passionfruit pulp
250g butter, softened
1 tablespoon finely grated lemon rind
1 cup (220g) caster sugar
3 eggs
1 cup (250ml) buttermilk
2 cups (300g) self-raising flour

LEMON SYRUP
⅓ cup (80ml) lemon juice
¼ cup (60ml) water
¾ cup (165g) caster sugar

1. Preheat oven to moderate (180°C/160°C fan-forced). Grease deep 19cm-square cake pan well; line base and sides with baking paper.
2. Strain passionfruit over medium jug; reserve both juice and seeds.
3. Beat butter, rind and sugar in small bowl with electric mixer until light and fluffy. Add eggs, one at a time, beating until combined between additions; transfer to large bowl.
4. Fold in combined passionfruit juice and buttermilk, and sifted flour, in two batches. Spread mixture into pan; bake about 1 hour.
5. Meanwhile, make lemon syrup.
6. Stand cake 5 minutes; turn, top-side up, onto wire rack set over tray. Pour hot syrup over hot cake; serve warm.

LEMON SYRUP Combine juice, the water, sugar and half of the reserved passionfruit seeds (discard remaining seeds or freeze for future use) in small saucepan; stir over heat, without boiling, until sugar dissolves. Simmer, uncovered, without stirring, 5 minutes.

Native to Australia, buttery, rich macadamia nuts have a high fat content and should be kept, covered, in the refrigerator to prevent them becoming rancid. You can blend or process the same weight of other roasted nuts, such as pecans, almonds or walnuts, if you prefer, to use in place of the macadamias. Similarly, you can substitute the same weight of other citrus fruit – grapefruits, blood oranges, tangelos, etc – for the mandarins.

mandarin, polenta and macadamia cake

PREPARATION TIME **20 MINUTES (PLUS COOLING TIME)** COOKING TIME **2 HOURS (PLUS STANDING TIME)**

4 small mandarins (400g), unpeeled
2 cups (280g) macadamias
250g butter, softened
1 teaspoon vanilla extract
1 cup (220g) caster sugar

3 eggs
1 cup (170g) polenta
1 teaspoon baking powder
1 tablespoon icing sugar

1. Cover whole mandarins in medium saucepan with cold water; bring to a boil. Drain then repeat process two more times. Cool mandarins to room temperature.

2. Preheat oven to moderately slow (170°C/150°C fan-forced). Grease deep 22cm-round cake pan; line base with baking paper.

3. Blend or process nuts until mixture forms a coarse meal. Halve mandarins; discard seeds. Blend or process mandarins until pulpy.

4. Beat butter, extract and caster sugar in small bowl with electric mixer until light and fluffy. Add eggs, one at a time, beating until just combined between additions; transfer to large bowl. Stir in polenta, baking powder, nut meal and mandarin pulp.

5. Spread mixture into pan; bake about 1 hour. Stand cake 15 minutes; turn, top-side up, onto wire rack to cool. Serve cake dusted with sifted icing sugar.

Use whatever coffee-flavoured liqueur you prefer in the mascarpone cream filling, or consider using chocolate, almond or hazelnut, licorice or even mint liqueur. Tia Maria, Kahlúa, Vandermint, crème de cacao, crème de menthe, Sambuca, Amaretto, Frangelico – any of these would work well here. This roulade uses plain rather than self-raising flour; its rising is thanks to the air incorporated into the three eggs.

tiramisu roulade

PREPARATION TIME **35 MINUTES** COOKING TIME **20 MINUTES (PLUS REFRIGERATION TIME)**

2 tablespoons coffee-flavoured liqueur
¼ cup (60ml) water
2 tablespoons caster sugar
1 tablespoon instant coffee granules
1 tablespoon boiling water
3 eggs
½ cup (110g) caster sugar, extra

½ cup (75g) plain flour
2 tablespoons flaked almonds

COFFEE LIQUEUR CREAM
1 cup (250g) mascarpone
½ cup (125ml) thickened cream
2 tablespoons coffee-flavoured liqueur

1. Preheat oven to hot (220°C/200°C fan-forced). Grease 25cm x 30cm swiss roll pan; line base and two long sides with baking paper, extending paper 5cm over long sides.

2. Combine liqueur with the water and sugar in small saucepan; bring to a boil. Reduce heat; simmer, uncovered, without stirring, about 5 minutes or until syrup thickens slightly. Remove from heat, stir in half of the coffee; reserve syrup.

3. Dissolve remaining coffee in the boiling water.

4. Beat eggs and extra sugar in small bowl with electric mixer about 5 minutes or until sugar is dissolved and mixture is thick; transfer to large bowl, fold in dissolved coffee.

5. Meanwhile, sift flour twice onto paper. Sift flour over egg mixture then fold gently into mixture. Spread sponge mixture into pan; sprinkle with almonds. Bake about 15 minutes.

6. Meanwhile, place a piece of baking paper cut the same size as swiss roll pan on bench; sprinkle evenly with about 2 teaspoons of caster sugar. Turn sponge onto sugared paper; peel away lining paper. Use serrated knife to cut crisp edges from all sides of sponge. Roll sponge from long side, using paper as guide; cool.

7. Meanwhile, beat ingredients for coffee liqueur cream in small bowl with electric mixer until firm peaks form. Unroll sponge, brush with reserved syrup. Spread cream over sponge then re-roll sponge. Cover roulade with plastic wrap; refrigerate 30 minutes before serving.

You will need approximately 2 large overripe bananas (460g) for this recipe. It is very important that the bananas you use are overripe; less-ripe ones won't mash easily and can cause the cake to be too heavy. A banana's natural starch is converted to sugar during the ripening process, and it's this natural sugar that contributes to the correct balance of ingredients. The cake also develops quite a thick crust because of this sugar content.

chocolate banana cake

PREPARATION TIME **25 MINUTES** COOKING TIME **1 HOUR 15 MINUTES**

⅔ cup (160ml) milk
2 teaspoons lemon juice
150g butter, softened
1 cup (220g) caster sugar
2 eggs
2 cups (300g) self-raising flour
½ teaspoon bicarbonate of soda
1 cup mashed banana
100g dark eating chocolate, grated finely

CREAMY CHOC FROSTING
200g dark eating chocolate
1 cup (160g) icing sugar
½ cup (120g) sour cream

1. Preheat oven to moderately slow (170°C/150°C fan-forced). Grease deep 22cm-round cake pan; line base with paper.
2. Combine milk and juice in small jug; stand 10 minutes.
3. Meanwhile, beat butter and sugar in small bowl with electric mixer until light and fluffy. Beat in eggs, one at a time, until just combined; transfer mixture to large bowl. Stir in sifted flour and soda, banana, milk mixture and chocolate.
4. Spread mixture into pan; bake about 1 hour 10 minutes. Stand cake 5 minutes; turn, top-side up, onto wire rack to cool.
5. Meanwhile, make creamy choc frosting; spread cold cake with frosting.

CREAMY CHOC FROSTING Melt chocolate in medium heatproof bowl over medium saucepan of simmering water; gradually stir in icing sugar and sour cream.

There are several varieties of pine tree that produce nuts large enough to be harvested for use in cooking, but the best are those from the stone pine, a tree grown around the Mediterranean. Shaped rather like an elongated torpedo, this particularly buttery pine nut is superior in flavour to the cheaper Asian-grown variety.

lemon sour cream cake

PREPARATION TIME 15 MINUTES   COOKING TIME 1 HOUR (PLUS COOLING TIME)

250g butter, softened
1 tablespoon finely grated lemon rind
2 cups (440g) caster sugar
6 eggs
¾ cup (180g) sour cream

2 cups (300g) plain flour
¼ cup (35g) self-raising flour
½ cup (80g) pine nuts
1 tablespoon demerara sugar
¼ cup (90g) honey

1. Preheat oven to moderately slow (170°C/150°C fan-forced). Grease deep 23cm-square cake pan; line base and two opposite sides with baking paper, extending paper 5cm over sides.

2. Beat butter, rind and caster sugar in medium bowl with electric mixer until light and fluffy. Add eggs, one at a time, beating until just combined between additions (mixture might separate at this stage, but will come together later). Stir in sour cream and sifted flours, in two batches. Spread mixture into pan; bake 15 minutes.

3. Meanwhile, combine pine nuts and demerara sugar in small bowl.

4. Carefully remove cake from oven; working quickly, sprinkle evenly with nut mixture, press gently into cake. Return cake to oven; bake further 45 minutes. Stand cake 5 minutes; turn, top-side up, onto wire rack.

5. Meanwhile, heat honey in small saucepan. Drizzle hot cake evenly with hot honey; cool before serving.

A scatter of white chocolate stars and Maltesers top this rich, dark cake, but you can let your imagination run riot with other chocolate decoration ideas. Cut after-dinner mints into triangles or shards and mix them among the stars. You can also replace the Maltesers with chocolate-covered nuts or dried fruits – try peanuts or raisins.

the chocoholic's chocolate cake

PREPARATION TIME **35 MINUTES** COOKING TIME **2 HOURS (PLUS COOLING, STANDING AND REFRIGERATION TIME)**

250g butter, chopped
1 tablespoon instant coffee granules
1½ cups (375ml) water
2 cups (440g) caster sugar
1 teaspoon vanilla extract
200g dark eating chocolate,
　chopped coarsely

2 eggs, beaten lightly
1½ cups (225g) self-raising flour
1 cup (150g) plain flour
¼ cup (25g) cocoa powder
⅓ cup (80ml) cream
180g white eating chocolate, melted
2 x 45g packets Maltesers

1. Preheat oven to slow (150°C/130°C fan-forced). Grease deep 19cm-square cake pan; line base and sides with baking paper.

2. Heat butter, coffee, the water, sugar, extract and half of the dark chocolate in large saucepan, stirring until smooth. Transfer to large bowl; cool 20 minutes. Stir in eggs and sifted dry ingredients.

3. Pour mixture into pan; bake about 1 hour 50 minutes. Stand cake 15 minutes; turn, top-side up, onto wire rack to cool.

4. Combine cream and remaining dark chocolate in small saucepan, stirring over low heat until ganache mixture is smooth. Cover; refrigerate 1 hour or until ganache is firm.

5. Spread white chocolate into 15cm x 20cm rectangle onto baking paper; stand until just set. Using 3cm- and 5cm-star cutter, cut as many stars as possible from white chocolate. Stand about 30 minutes or until firm.

6. Spread cake with ganache; decorate with stars and Maltesers.

Fresh as well as frozen blueberries can be used in this cake. Don't thaw the frozen fruit, however, because it's possible that the colour might bleed into the cake. The surface of the partially cooked cake should be flat and just set before sprinkling with blueberries, to ensure that the berries don't sink during the remaining baking time. The cake is best served warm, with crème fraîche, if desired.

olive oil cake with blueberries

PREPARATION TIME **25 MINUTES** COOKING TIME **1 HOUR**

3 eggs
1¼ cups (275g) caster sugar
2 tablespoons finely grated orange rind
½ cup (125ml) olive oil
⅓ cup (80ml) milk

1 cup (150g) plain flour
1 cup (150g) self-raising flour
100g frozen blueberries
¼ cup (80g) apricot jam,
  warmed, strained

1. Preheat oven to moderate (180°C/160°C fan-forced). Grease deep 19cm-square cake pan.
2. Beat eggs, sugar and rind in small bowl with electric mixer until sugar is dissolved; transfer to large bowl. Fold in combined oil and milk, and sifted flours, in two batches.
3. Pour mixture into pan; bake 20 minutes. Carefully remove cake from oven; sprinkle surface evenly with blueberries. Return cake to oven; bake about 40 minutes. Stand cake 10 minutes; turn, top-side up, onto wire rack to cool.
4. Brush warm cake with jam.

kumara and pecan loaf

PREPARATION TIME **20 MINUTES** COOKING TIME **1 HOUR 40 MINUTES**

200g butter, softened
¾ cup (165g) firmly packed brown sugar
2 eggs
¾ cup (90g) pecans, chopped coarsely

½ cup (40g) desiccated coconut
1 cup mashed kumara
1½ cups (225g) self-raising flour
½ cup (125ml) milk

1. Preheat oven to moderately slow (170°C/150°C fan-forced). Grease 14cm x 21cm loaf pan; line base and long sides with baking paper, extending paper 2cm over sides.
2. Beat butter, sugar and eggs in small bowl with electric mixer until just combined; transfer mixture to large bowl. Fold in nuts, coconut and kumara. Stir in sifted flour and milk, in two batches.
3. Spread mixture into pan; bake about 1 hour 40 minutes. Stand loaf 10 minutes; turn, top-side up, onto wire rack to cool.

Thanks to hothouse growing, rhubarb is available all year, so you can indulge in a hot pie or crumble as well as any number of luscious desserts matching rhubarb with berries and cream or mascarpone whenever you like. Be sure to discard every bit of the vegetable's leaf and use only the thinnest stalks (the thick ones tend to be stringy).

rhubarb and almond cakes

PREPARATION TIME **20 MINUTES**   COOKING TIME **40 MINUTES**

½ cup (125ml) milk
¼ cup (40g) blanched almonds, toasted
80g butter, softened
1 teaspoon vanilla extract
½ cup (110g) caster sugar
2 eggs
1 cup (150g) self-raising flour

POACHED RHUBARB
250g trimmed rhubarb,
  chopped coarsely
¼ cup (60ml) water
½ cup (110g) white sugar

1. Preheat oven to moderate (180°C/160°C fan-forced). Grease a 6-hole texas (¾-cup/180ml) muffin pan.
2. Make poached rhubarb.
3. Meanwhile, blend or process milk and nuts until smooth.
4. Beat butter, extract and sugar in small bowl with electric mixer until light and fluffy. Add eggs, one at a time, beating until just combined between additions (mixture might separate at this stage, but will come together later); transfer to large bowl. Stir in sifted flour and almond mixture.
5. Spoon mixture equally among muffin pan holes; bake 10 minutes. Carefully remove muffin pan from oven; divide drained rhubarb over muffins, bake further 15 minutes.
6. Stand muffins 5 minutes; turn, top-side up, onto wire rack to cool. Serve warm or cold with rhubarb syrup.

POACHED RHUBARB Place ingredients in medium saucepan; bring to a boil. Reduce heat; simmer, uncovered, about 10 minutes or until rhubarb is just tender. Drain rhubarb over medium bowl; reserve rhubarb and syrup separately.

The golden ginger cream served with this cake gets its distinctive taste from golden syrup, a liquid sweetener made from sugar cane juice. This syrup is mostly used in baking for making biscuits and cakes, and for fudge and toffee sauces to pour over ice-cream. It can also be used as you would honey or maple syrup, poured over waffles or pancakes.

fresh ginger cake with golden ginger cream

PREPARATION TIME **15 MINUTES** COOKING TIME **1 HOUR**

250g butter, chopped
½ cup (110g) firmly packed brown sugar
⅔ cup (230g) golden syrup
12cm piece fresh ginger (60g),
  grated finely
1 cup (150g) plain flour
1 cup (150g) self-raising flour
½ teaspoon bicarbonate of soda

2 eggs, beaten lightly
¾ cup (180ml) thickened cream

GOLDEN GINGER CREAM
300ml thickened cream
2 tablespoons golden syrup
2 teaspoons ground ginger

1. Preheat oven to moderate (180°C/160°C fan-forced). Grease deep 22cm-round cake pan.

2. Melt butter in medium saucepan; add sugar, syrup and ginger. Stir over low heat until sugar dissolves.

3. Whisk in combined sifted flours and soda then egg and cream. Pour mixture into pan; bake about 50 minutes. Stand cake 10 minutes; turn, top-side up, onto wire rack to cool.

4. Meanwhile, beat golden ginger cream ingredients in small bowl with electric mixer until soft peaks form. Serve cake with cream.

Grate the citrus rind called for here then save the fruit to extract the juice for another use. Without this protective "skin", the fruit will become dry and hard, so they should be juiced, say for a salsa or salad dressing, within a day or two.

lemon and lime white chocolate mud cake

PREPARATION TIME **20 MINUTES** COOKING TIME **1 HOUR 50 MINUTES (PLUS COOLING AND REFRIGERATION TIME)**

250g butter, chopped
2 teaspoons finely grated lemon rind
2 teaspoons finely grated lime rind
180g white eating chocolate,
  chopped coarsely
1½ cups (330g) caster sugar
¾ cup (180ml) milk
1½ cups (225g) plain flour
½ cup (75g) self-raising flour
2 eggs, beaten lightly

COCONUT GANACHE
140ml can coconut cream
360g white eating chocolate,
  chopped finely
1 teaspoon finely grated lemon rind
1 teaspoon finely grated lime rind

1. Preheat oven to moderately slow (170°C/150°C fan-forced). Grease deep 20cm-round cake pan; line base with baking paper.
2. Combine butter, rinds, chocolate, sugar and milk in medium saucepan; stir over low heat until smooth. Transfer mixture to large bowl; cool 15 minutes.
3. Stir in sifted flours and egg; pour mixture into pan. Bake about 1 hour 40 minutes; cool cake in pan.
4. Meanwhile, make coconut ganache.
5. Turn cake, top-side up, onto serving plate; spread ganache over cake.

COCONUT GANACHE Bring coconut cream to a boil in small saucepan; combine chocolate and rinds in medium bowl. Add hot cream; stir until smooth. Cover bowl; refrigerate, stirring occasionally, about 30 minutes or until ganache is spreadable.

Make sure that the bananas you choose to mash for the cake mixture are overripe; if they're not, they won't mash easily and can cause the cake to be too heavy. We prefer to use an underproof rum in baking because of its more subtle flavour; however, you can use an overproof rum and still get satisfactory results.

upside-down toffee date and banana cake

PREPARATION TIME **20 MINUTES** COOKING TIME **1 HOUR 10 MINUTES**

1½ cups (330g) caster sugar
1½ cups (375ml) water
3 star anise
2 medium bananas (400g), sliced thinly
1 cup (140g) dried seeded dates
¾ cup (180ml) water, extra
½ cup (125ml) dark rum
1 teaspoon bicarbonate of soda

60g butter, chopped
½ cup (110g) firmly packed brown sugar
2 eggs
2 teaspoons mixed spice
1 cup (150g) self-raising flour
½ cup mashed banana
300ml thickened cream

1. Preheat oven to moderate (180°C/160°C fan-forced). Grease deep 22cm-round cake pan; line base with baking paper.
2. Stir caster sugar, the water and star anise in medium saucepan over low heat, without boiling, until sugar dissolves. Bring to a boil; boil syrup, uncovered, without stirring, about 5 minutes or until thickened slightly. Strain ½ cup of the syrup into small heatproof jug; reserve to flavour cream. Discard star-anise.
3. To make toffee, continue boiling remaining syrup, uncovered, without stirring, about 10 minutes or until toffee is golden brown. Pour hot toffee into cake pan; top with sliced banana.
4. Combine dates, the extra water and rum in small saucepan; bring to a boil then remove from heat. Stir in soda; stand 5 minutes. Blend or process date mixture with butter and brown sugar until almost smooth. Add eggs, spice and flour; blend or process until just combined. Stir in mashed banana.
5. Pour mixture into pan; bake about 40 minutes. Turn cake, in pan, onto serving plate; stand 2 minutes. Remove pan then baking paper.
6. To make star anise cream, beat cream in small bowl with electric mixer until firm peaks form. Stir in reserved syrup.
7. Serve cake warm or at room temperature with star anise cream.

brown sugar sponge

PREPARATION TIME **30 MINUTES** COOKING TIME **20 MINUTES (PLUS COOLING TIME)**

4 eggs
¾ cup (165g) firmly packed
  dark brown sugar
1 cup (150g) wheaten cornflour
1 teaspoon cream of tartar
½ teaspoon bicarbonate of soda
300ml thickened cream

PRALINE
⅓ cup (75g) white sugar
¼ cup (60ml) water
½ teaspoon malt vinegar
⅓ cup (45g) roasted hazelnuts

1. Preheat oven to moderate (180°C/160°C fan-forced). Grease two deep 22cm-round cake pans.
2. Beat eggs and brown sugar in small bowl with electric mixer about 10 minutes or until thick and creamy; transfer to large bowl.
3. Sift cornflour, cream of tartar and soda twice onto paper then sift over egg mixture; gently fold dry ingredients into egg mixture. Divide mixture between pans; bake about 18 minutes. Turn sponges immediately onto baking-paper-covered wire racks to cool.
4. Meanwhile, make praline.
5. Beat cream in small bowl with electric mixer until firm peaks form; fold in praline. Place one sponge on serving plate; spread with half of the cream mixture. Top with remaining sponge; spread with remaining cream mixture.

PRALINE Stir sugar, the water and vinegar in small saucepan over heat, without boiling, until sugar dissolves; bring to a boil. Reduce heat; simmer, uncovered, without stirring, about 10 minutes or until syrup is golden brown. Add hazelnuts; pour praline mixture onto baking-paper-covered tray. Cool about 15 minutes or until set. Break praline into pieces then blend or process until mixture is as fine (or coarse) as desired.

marbled chocolate mud cake

PREPARATION TIME **25 MINUTES** COOKING TIME **1 HOUR**

250g butter, softened
1 teaspoon vanilla extract
1¼ cups (275g) caster sugar
3 eggs
2¼ cups (335g) self-raising flour
¾ cup (180ml) buttermilk
¼ cup (25g) cocoa powder
¼ cup (60ml) milk
½ cup (95g) white Choc Bits
½ cup (95g) dark Choc Bits

CHOCOLATE BUTTER CREAM
125g butter, softened
1½ cups (240g) icing sugar
2 tablespoons milk
2 tablespoons cocoa powder

1. Preheat oven to moderate (180°C/160°C fan-forced). Grease deep 22cm-round cake pan; line base with baking paper.
2. Beat butter, extract and sugar in small bowl with electric mixer until light and fluffy. Add eggs, one at a time, beating until just combined between additions; transfer mixture to large bowl. Stir in sifted flour and buttermilk, in two batches.
3. Divide cake mixture between two bowls. Blend sifted cocoa with milk; stir into one of the bowls of mixture with white Choc Bits. Stir dark Choc Bits into remaining mixture.
4. Drop alternate spoonfuls of mixtures into pan, then pull skewer back and forth through cake mixture several times to achieve a marbled effect. Bake cake about 1 hour. Stand cake 5 minutes; turn, top-side up, onto wire rack to cool.
5. Meanwhile, make chocolate butter cream.
6. Drop alternate spoonfuls of the two butter cream mixtures onto cake; spread over top and side of cake.

CHOCOLATE BUTTER CREAM Beat butter in small bowl with electric mixer until light and fluffy. Gradually beat in half of the icing sugar, then the milk, then the remaining icing sugar. Transfer half of the mixture to another small bowl; stir sifted cocoa into one of the bowls.

Grate the lemon for the frosting before you extract the fruit's juice for the cake mixture. Essential oils within the rind add a concentrated burst of lemony zing to the mascarpone and cream used in the frosting – and help make this homely cake really something special.

lemon cake

PREPARATION TIME **20 MINUTES** COOKING TIME **1 HOUR**

125g butter, softened
2 teaspoons finely grated lemon rind
1¼ cups (275g) caster sugar
3 eggs
1½ cups (225g) self-raising flour
½ cup (125ml) milk
¼ cup (60ml) lemon juice

LEMON MASCARPONE FROSTING
300ml thickened cream
½ cup icing sugar
2 teaspoons finely grated lemon rind
150g mascarpone

1. Preheat oven to moderate (180°C/160°C fan-forced). Grease deep 20cm-round cake pan; line base with baking paper.
2. Make lemon mascarpone frosting. Refrigerate, covered, until required.
3. Beat butter, rind and sugar in small bowl with electric mixer until light and fluffy. Add eggs, one at a time, beating until just combined between additions (mixture might separate at this stage, but will come together later); transfer mixture to large bowl. Stir in sifted flour, milk and juice, in two batches.
4. Pour mixture into pan; bake about 50 minutes. Stand cake 5 minutes; turn, top-side up, onto wire rack to cool.
5. Split cold cake into three layers, place one layer onto serving plate, cut-side up; spread with one-third of the frosting. Repeat layering process, finishing with frosting.

LEMON MASCARPONE FROSTING Beat cream, sifted icing sugar and rind in small bowl with electric mixer until soft peaks form. Fold cream mixture into mascarpone.

Chopping the raisins, dates and prunes to a similar size as the sultanas will make the finished cake cut better. This rich fruit cake will keep indefinitely if stored in an airtight container in a clean cool, dark place, or in the refrigerator or freezer.

boiled whisky fruit cake

PREPARATION TIME 35 MINUTES COOKING TIME **3 HOURS (PLUS STANDING TIME)**

1½ cups (250g) raisins
1½ cups (210g) dried seeded dates
1½ cups (250g) seeded prunes
1½ cups (250g) sultanas
⅓ cup (70g) red glacé
  cherries, quartered
⅓ cup (55g) mixed peel
2 tablespoons caster sugar
30g butter
½ cup (125ml) whisky

250g butter, chopped, extra
1 cup (220g) firmly packed dark
  brown sugar
½ teaspoon bicarbonate of soda
½ cup (70g) slivered almonds
2 cups (300g) plain flour
2 teaspoons mixed spice
5 eggs
¼ cup (60ml) whisky, extra

1. Chop raisins, dates and prunes the same size as the sultanas; combine in a large bowl with sultanas, cherries and peel.
2. Place caster sugar in large heavy-based saucepan over medium heat; turn pan occasionally until sugar is melted. Add butter and whisky; stir over low heat until smooth.
3. Add extra butter, brown sugar and fruit to pan. Stir over heat until butter melts; bring to a boil. Remove from heat; stir in soda. Transfer to large bowl, cover; stand overnight at room temperature.
4. Preheat oven to slow (150°C/130°C fan-forced). Grease deep 19cm-square cake pan; line base and sides with 2 layers of brown paper then baking paper, extending paper 5cm over sides.
5. Add nuts, sifted flour and spice, and eggs to fruit mixture; stir until well combined.
6. Spoon mixture into corners of pan then spread remaining mixture into pan. Drop pan from a height of about 15cm onto bench to settle mixture into pan and to break any large air bubbles; level surface of cake with wet spatula.
7. Bake cake about 3 hours.
8. Brush hot cake with extra whisky. Cover hot cake tightly with foil; cool in pan.

The three types of nuts used here are tossed with the spice mixture then toasted, a process that infuses the cake with their combined flavours. The secret to a successful teacake lies in the beating of the sugar, egg and butter – the mixture must be very light in colour and full of air.

spices of the orient teacake

PREPARATION TIME **20 MINUTES**   COOKING TIME **25 MINUTES**

60g butter, softened
1 teaspoon vanilla extract
½ cup (110g) caster sugar
1 egg
1 cup (150g) self-raising flour
⅓ cup (80ml) milk
20g butter, melted, extra

SPICED NUTS
2 tablespoons shelled pistachios, chopped finely
2 tablespoons blanched almonds, chopped finely
2 tablespoons pine nuts, chopped finely
¼ cup (40g) icing sugar
½ teaspoon ground allspice
½ teaspoon ground cardamom
1 teaspoon ground cinnamon

1. Preheat oven to moderate (180°C/160°C fan-forced). Grease 20cm-round cake pan.
2. Beat butter, extract, sugar and egg in small bowl with electric mixer until light and fluffy. Stir in sifted flour and milk.
3. Spread mixture into pan; bake about 25 minutes. Stand cake 5 minutes; turn, top-side up, onto wire rack to cool.
4. Meanwhile, make spiced nuts.
5. Brush cooled cake with extra butter; sprinkle with spiced nuts. Serve warm.

SPICED NUTS Place nuts in strainer; rinse under cold water. Combine wet nuts in large bowl with icing sugar and spices; spread mixture onto oven tray, toast in moderate oven about 10 minutes or until nuts are dry.

mini chocolate hazelnut cakes

PREPARATION TIME **35 MINUTES** COOKING TIME **25 MINUTES (PLUS STANDING TIME)**

- -

100g dark eating chocolate,
  chopped coarsely
¾ cup (180ml) water
100g butter, softened
1 cup (220g) firmly packed brown sugar
3 eggs
¼ cup (25g) cocoa powder
¾ cup (110g) self-raising flour
⅓ cup (35g) hazelnut meal

WHIPPED HAZELNUT GANACHE
⅓ cup (80ml) thickened cream
180g milk eating chocolate,
  chopped finely
2 tablespoons hazelnut-flavoured liqueur

1. Preheat oven to moderate (180°C/160°C fan-forced). Grease twelve ½-cup (125ml) oval friand pans.

2. Make whipped hazelnut ganache.

3. Meanwhile, combine chocolate and the water in medium saucepan; stir over low heat until smooth.

4. Beat butter and sugar in small bowl with electric mixer until light and fluffy. Add eggs, one at a time, beating until just combined between additions (mixture might separate at this stage, but will come together later); transfer mixture to medium bowl. Stir in warm chocolate mixture, sifted cocoa and flour, and hazelnut meal.

5. Divide mixture among pans; bake about 20 minutes. Stand cakes 5 minutes; turn, top-sides up, onto wire rack to cool. Spread ganache over cakes.

WHIPPED HAZELNUT GANACHE Combine cream and chocolate in small saucepan; stir over low heat until smooth. Stir in liqueur; transfer mixture to small bowl. Cover; stand about 2 hours or until just firm. Beat ganache in small bowl with electric mixer until mixture changes to a pale brown colour.

Ginger wine, a beverage that is 14% alcohol by volume, has the piquant taste of fresh ginger. You can substitute it with dry (white) vermouth, if you prefer. Any type or combination of glacé fruit can be used in this recipe.

glacé fruit cake

PREPARATION TIME **20 MINUTES** COOKING TIME **2 HOURS 30 MINUTES**

185g butter, softened
½ cup (110g) caster sugar
3 eggs
1 cup (250g) finely chopped glacé apricot
½ cup (80g) finely chopped glacé orange
½ cup (90g) finely chopped glacé ginger
¾ cup (210g) finely chopped glacé fig

1½ cups (225g) plain flour
½ cup (75g) self-raising flour
½ cup (125ml) milk
¼ cup (60ml) ginger wine

GINGER SYRUP
¼ cup (60ml) ginger wine
¼ cup (60ml) water
¼ cup (55g) caster sugar
2 teaspoons lemon juice

1. Preheat oven to slow (150°C/130°C fan-forced). Line the base and both long sides of 14cm x 21cm loaf pan with baking paper, extending paper 5cm above sides.
2. Beat butter and sugar in small bowl with electric mixer until just combined. Add eggs, one at a time, beating until just combined between additions; transfer to large bowl. Stir in fruit then sifted flours, and combined milk and wine, in two batches. Spread mixture into pan; bake about 2 hours 30 minutes.
3. Meanwhile, make ginger syrup.
4. Pour hot ginger syrup over hot cake in pan. Cover cake with foil; cool in pan.

GINGER SYRUP Stir ingredients in small saucepan over low heat, without boiling, until sugar dissolves; bring to a boil. Boil, uncovered, without stirring, about 2 minutes or until syrup thickens slightly.

Matzo meal can be found in some supermarkets and delicatessens. If you can't find it, make your own by processing matzo crackers, biscuit-like unleavened bread, found in boxes on most supermarket shelves. It's important to use regular honey in the matzo cake, not the easy-to-pour liquefied version.

matzo honey cake

PREPARATION TIME **15 MINUTES** COOKING TIME **40 MINUTES**

3 eggs, separated
1½ cups (180g) matzo meal
2 teaspoons finely grated orange rind
¼ teaspoon ground clove
1 teaspoon ground cinnamon

⅔ cup (160ml) orange juice
¾ cup (270g) honey
½ cup (110g) firmly packed brown sugar
1 tablespoon icing sugar

1. Preheat oven to moderate (180°C/160°C fan-forced). Grease base of deep 22cm-round cake pan; line base with baking paper.
2. Combine egg yolks, matzo, rind, spices, juice, honey and brown sugar in large bowl.
3. Beat egg whites in small bowl with electric mixer until soft peaks form; fold into matzo mixture, in two batches.
4. Pour cake mixture into pan; bake about 40 minutes. Stand cake 5 minutes; turn, top-side up, onto wire rack to cool.
5. Serve dusted with sifted icing sugar.

gluten-free berry cupcakes

PREPARATION TIME **20 MINUTES** COOKING TIME **25 MINUTES**

125g butter, softened
2 teaspoons finely grated lemon rind
¾ cup (165g) caster sugar
4 eggs
2 cups (240g) almond meal

½ cup (40g) desiccated coconut
½ cup (100g) rice flour
1 teaspoon bicarbonate of soda
1 cup (150g) frozen mixed berries
1 tablespoon desiccated coconut, extra

1. Preheat oven to moderate (180°C/160°C fan-forced). Grease 12-hole (⅓-cup/80ml) muffin pan.
2. Beat butter, rind and sugar in small bowl with electric mixer until light and fluffy. Add eggs, one at a time, beating until just combined between additions (mixture will separate at this stage, but will come together later); transfer to large bowl. Stir in almond meal, coconut, sifted flour and soda, then the berries.
3. Divide mixture among muffin pan holes; bake about 25 minutes. Stand cupcakes 5 minutes; turn, top-sides up, onto wire rack to cool. Sprinkle with extra coconut.

A fortified wine, like sherry and port, muscat is the result of grapes left to ripen well beyond normal harvesting time, resulting in a concentrated dark, toffee-coloured wine with a rich yet mellow flavour, equally good used in cooking as it is as an after-dinner drink.

muscat prune shortcake

PREPARATION TIME **30 MINUTES** COOKING TIME **25 MINUTES (PLUS COOLING AND REFRIGERATION TIME)**

200g butter, softened
1 teaspoon finely grated lemon rind
⅓ cup (75g) caster sugar
¼ cup (50g) rice flour
¾ cup (110g) self-raising flour
¾ cup (110g) plain flour
300ml thickened cream
1 tablespoon caster sugar, extra

MUSCAT PRUNES
1 cup (170g) seeded prunes,
  chopped coarsely
1 cup (250ml) muscat

1. Preheat oven to moderate (180°C/160°C fan-forced). Grease three 20cm-round sandwich pans.
2. Beat butter, rind and sugar in medium bowl with electric mixer until light and fluffy. Fold in sifted flours, in two batches.
3. Press mixture evenly into pans; bake about 20 minutes. Stand shortcakes in pans; cool to room temperature.
4. Meanwhile, make muscat prunes.
5. Beat cream in small bowl with electric mixer until firm peaks form. Place one shortcake into deep 20cm-round cake pan or 20cm springform tin; spread with half of the prune mixture then half of the whipped cream. Top with another shortcake; spread with remaining prune mixture then remaining whipped cream. Top with remaining shortcake, cover; refrigerate overnight.
6. Remove from pan; serve sprinkled with extra sugar.

MUSCAT PRUNES Stir prunes and muscat in small saucepan over heat, without boiling, until prunes soften. Cool to room temperature.

Just as you do when making a traditional sticky date pudding, soften the dates by standing them for several minutes in bicarbonate of soda dissolved in boiling water. For the most flavourful results, always use pure maple syrup rather than maple-flavoured syrup when making this recipe.

date and maple loaf

PREPARATION TIME **20 MINUTES** COOKING TIME **50 MINUTES**

¾ cup (110g) finely chopped
  seeded dates
⅓ cup (80ml) boiling water
½ teaspoon bicarbonate of soda
¼ cup (90g) maple syrup
90g butter, softened
⅓ cup (75g) firmly packed
  brown sugar

2 eggs
¾ cup (120g) wholemeal
  self-raising flour
½ cup (75g) plain flour

MAPLE BUTTER
125g butter, softened
2 tablespoons maple syrup

1. Preheat oven to moderate (180°C/160°C fan-forced). Grease 14cm x 21cm loaf pan.
2. Combine dates and the water in small heatproof bowl. Stir in soda; stand 5 minutes. Stir in maple syrup.
3. Meanwhile, beat butter and sugar in medium bowl with electric mixer until light and fluffy. Add eggs, one at a time, beating until just combined between additions (mixture will separate at this stage, but will come together later). Add butter mixture to date mixture; stir in sifted flours, in two batches.
4. Spread mixture into pan; bake about 50 minutes. Stand loaf in pan 10 minutes; turn, top-side up, onto wire rack to cool.
5. Meanwhile, whisk ingredients for maple butter in small bowl until combined. Serve loaf warm or cold with maple butter.

Make a long, fairly wide pleat in the foil covering the pan to allow the fruit loaf to expand during baking. Use a full cream plain yogurt and not a light or low-fat variation in the mixture to ensure the quality of the finished product.

yogurt fruit loaf

PREPARATION TIME **20 MINUTES**   COOKING TIME **1 HOUR 30 MINUTES**

100g butter, softened
2 teaspoons finely grated orange rind
¾ cup (165g) caster sugar
2 eggs
2 cups (320g) wholemeal
  self-raising flour

1 cup (280g) yogurt
⅓ cup (80ml) orange juice
1 cup (200g) finely chopped dried figs
1 cup (150g) coarsely chopped raisins

1. Preheat oven to moderate (180°C/160°C fan-forced). Grease 14cm x 21cm loaf pan.
2. Beat butter, rind, sugar, eggs, flour, yogurt and juice in medium bowl with electric mixer, on low speed, until just combined. Stir in fruit.
3. Pour mixture into pan; cover with foil. Bake 1 hour 15 minutes; remove foil, bake about a further 15 minutes. Stand loaf 10 minutes; turn, top-side up, onto wire rack to cool. Serve at room temperature or toasted, with butter.

Both the carrot and the almond are thought to have come from North Africa and they have a flavour affinity that suits their being combined, both in savoury dishes and in baking. And there may be no sweeter example of this than this easy-to-make and good-keeping cake.

almond carrot cake

PREPARATION TIME **20 MINUTES** COOKING TIME **1 HOUR 15 MINUTES**

5 eggs, separated
1 teaspoon finely grated lemon rind
1¼ cups (275g) caster sugar
2 cups (480g) coarsely grated carrot
2 cups (240g) almond meal
½ cup (75g) self-raising flour
2 tablespoons toasted slivered almonds

CREAM CHEESE FROSTING
100g packaged cream cheese, softened
80g butter, softened
½ cup (80g) icing sugar
1 teaspoon lemon juice

1. Preheat oven to moderate (180°C/160°C fan-forced). Grease deep 19cm-square cake pan; line base with baking paper.
2. Beat egg yolks, rind and sugar in small bowl with electric mixer until thick and creamy; transfer to large bowl. Stir in carrot, almond meal and sifted flour.
3. Beat egg whites in small bowl with electric mixer until soft peaks form; fold into carrot mixture in two batches.
4. Pour mixture into pan; bake about 1 hour 15 minutes. Stand cake 5 minutes; turn, top-side up, onto wire rack to cool.
5. Meanwhile, make cream cheese frosting.
6. Spread cold cake with cream cheese frosting; sprinkle with slivered almonds.

CREAM CHEESE FROSTING Beat cream cheese and butter in small bowl with electric mixer until light and fluffy; gradually beat in icing sugar and juice.

almond honey spice cake

PREPARATION TIME **20 MINUTES** COOKING TIME **40 MINUTES (PLUS COOLING, REFRIGERATION AND STANDING TIME)**

125g butter, softened
⅓ cup (75g) caster sugar
2 tablespoons honey
1 teaspoon ground ginger
1 teaspoon ground allspice
2 eggs
1½ cups (180g) almond meal
½ cup (80g) semolina
1 teaspoon baking powder
¼ cup (60ml) milk

SPICED SYRUP
1 cup (220g) caster sugar
1 cup (250ml) water
8 cardamom pods, bruised
2 cinnamon sticks

HONEY ORANGE CREAM
¾ cup (180ml) thickened cream
1 tablespoon honey
2 tablespoons finely grated orange rind

1. Preheat oven to moderate (180°C/160°C fan-forced). Grease deep 20cm-round cake pan; line base and side with baking paper.

2. Beat butter, sugar, honey and spices in small bowl with electric mixer until light and fluffy. Add eggs, one at a time, beating until just combined between additions; transfer mixture to medium bowl. Fold in almond meal, semolina, baking powder and milk.

3. Spread mixture into pan; bake about 40 minutes. Stand cake 5 minutes.

4. Meanwhile, make spiced syrup.

5. Pour strained hot syrup over hot cake in pan; cool cake in pan to room temperature. Turn cake, in pan, upside-down onto serving plate; refrigerate 3 hours or overnight.

6. Remove cake from refrigerator. Make honey orange cream. Remove pan from cake; serve cake at room temperature with honey orange cream.

SPICED SYRUP Stir ingredients in small saucepan over heat, without boiling, until sugar dissolves; bring to a boil. Boil, uncovered, without stirring, about 5 minutes or until syrup thickens slightly.

HONEY ORANGE CREAM Beat cream, honey and rind in small bowl with electric mixer until soft peaks form.

The Aztecs first combined chocolate and chilli about 2600 years ago, and the tradition has continued in contemporary Mexican cooking in the mole, a sauce that confirms the harmony between these two foods. Eating the chilli cherries with bites of this rich dark cake will confirm that the two tastes do indeed complement one another. Use your favourite whisky instead of bourbon, if you prefer. Fresh or canned cherries can replace the frozen variety, if necessary. Use the drained cherries' syrup to replace an equal amount of the required two cups of water.

chocolate mud cake with chilli cherries

PREPARATION TIME **25 MINUTES** COOKING TIME **1 HOUR 35 MINUTES (PLUS COOLING TIME)**

250g butter, chopped
200g dark eating chocolate,
  chopped coarsely
2 cups (440g) caster sugar
1 cup (250ml) milk
1 teaspoon vanilla extract
⅓ cup (80ml) bourbon
1½ cups (225g) plain flour
¼ cup (35g) self-raising flour
¼ cup (25g) cocoa powder
2 eggs

DARK CHOCOLATE GANACHE
⅓ cup (80ml) cream
200g dark eating chocolate

CHILLI CHERRIES
2 cups (500ml) water
¾ cup (165g) caster sugar
1 fresh red thai chilli, halved lengthways
1 star anise
6 whole black peppercorns
10cm piece orange peel
300g frozen cherries

1. Preheat oven to moderately slow (170°C/150°C fan-forced). Grease deep 22cm-round cake pan; line base with baking paper.
2. Combine butter, chocolate, sugar, milk, extract and bourbon in medium saucepan; stir over low heat until smooth. Transfer to large bowl; cool 15 minutes. Whisk in sifted flours and cocoa, then eggs.
3. Pour mixture into pan; bake about 1 hour 30 minutes.
4. Meanwhile, make chilli cherries.
5. Stand cake 5 minutes; turn, top-side up, onto wire rack to cool.
6. Meanwhile, make dark chocolate ganache by bringing cream to a boil in small saucepan. Remove from heat; add chocolate, stir until smooth.
7. Spread cold cake with ganache; serve with chilli cherries.

CHILLI CHERRIES Stir the water, sugar, chilli, star anise, peppercorns and peel in medium saucepan over low heat, without boiling, until sugar dissolves. Bring to a boil; boil 2 minutes. Add cherries; simmer 5 minutes or until cherries are just tender. Cool cherries in syrup. Remove cherries from pan; bring syrup to a boil. Boil 10 minutes or until syrup thickens slightly; cool. Return cherries to pan.

In this recipe, cream replaces milk and butter, resulting in a cake that's firm like a buttercake – even though it's made like a sponge.

whipped cream cake with caramel icing

PREPARATION TIME **20 MINUTES** COOKING TIME **50 MINUTES**

600ml thickened cream
3 eggs
1 teaspoon vanilla extract
1¼ cups (275g) firmly packed
  brown sugar
2 cups (300g) self-raising flour

CARAMEL ICING
60g butter
½ cup (110g) firmly packed brown sugar
2 tablespoons milk
½ cup (80g) icing sugar

1. Preheat oven to moderate (180°C/160°C fan-forced). Grease deep 22cm-round cake pan; line base with baking paper.
2. Beat half of the cream in small bowl with electric mixer until soft peaks form. Beat eggs and extract in small bowl with electric mixer until thick and creamy; gradually add sugar, beating until dissolved between additions.
3. Transfer mixture to large bowl. Fold in a quarter of the whipped cream then sifted flour, then remaining whipped cream. Spread into pan; bake about 50 minutes. Stand cake 5 minutes; turn, top-side up, onto wire rack to cool.
4. Meanwhile, beat remaining cream in small bowl with electric mixer until firm peaks form.
5. Make caramel icing.
6. Split cold cake in half; sandwich layers with cream. Spread cake with caramel icing.

CARAMEL ICING Melt butter in small saucepan, add brown sugar and milk; bring to a boil. Reduce heat immediately; simmer 2 minutes. Cool to room temperature. Stir in icing sugar until smooth.

We used the Golden Delicious variety for this recipe, a crisp, almost citrus-coloured apple with excellent flavour and good keeping properties. It's probably the best cooking apple around, but you can substitute it with green-skinned Granny Smiths if you prefer.

caramelised apple buttercake

PREPARATION TIME **20 MINUTES** COOKING TIME **1 HOUR**

2 medium apples (300g)
80g butter
¾ cup (165g) firmly packed brown sugar
125g butter, softened, extra
⅔ cup (150g) caster sugar
1 teaspoon vanilla extract

2 eggs
1 cup (150g) self-raising flour
⅔ cup (100g) plain flour
½ teaspoon bicarbonate of soda
1 cup (250ml) buttermilk
¾ cup (180ml) cream

1. Preheat oven to moderate (180°C/160°C fan-forced). Grease 20cm bundt pan.
2. Peel, core and quarter apples; slice thinly. Melt butter in large frying pan; cook apple about 5 minutes or until browned lightly. Add brown sugar; cook, stirring, about 5 minutes or until mixture thickens slightly. Strain apples over medium bowl. Reserve apples and cooking liquid.
3. Beat extra butter, caster sugar and extract in small bowl with electric mixer until light and fluffy. Add eggs, one at a time, beating until just combined between additions; transfer to large bowl. Stir in sifted dry ingredients and buttermilk, in two batches.
4. Spread two-thirds of the mixture into pan. Top with apples, leaving a 2cm border around the edge; cover with remaining mixture. Bake about 50 minutes. Stand cake 5 minutes; turn, top-side up, onto wire rack to cool.
5. Meanwhile, return reserved apple liquid to large frying pan, add cream; bring to a boil. Reduce heat; simmer, uncovered, about 15 minutes or until sauce thickens.
6. Serve warm cake with caramel sauce.

quince and blackberry crumble cake

PREPARATION TIME **30 MINUTES** COOKING TIME **2 HOURS 15 MINUTES (PLUS COOLING TIME)**

185g unsalted butter, softened
¾ cup (165g) caster sugar
2 eggs
2¼ cups (335g) self-raising flour
¾ cup (180ml) milk
2 cups (300g) frozen blackberries
2 teaspoons cornflour

POACHED QUINCE
3 cups (750ml) water
¾ cup (165g) caster sugar
1 cinnamon stick
1 tablespoon lemon juice
3 medium quinces (1kg),
  each cut into 8 wedges

CINNAMON CRUMBLE
¾ cup (110g) plain flour
2 tablespoons caster sugar
½ cup (110g) firmly packed brown sugar
100g cold unsalted butter, chopped
1 teaspoon ground cinnamon

1. Make poached quince.
2. Preheat oven to moderate (180°C/160°C fan-forced). Grease deep 23cm-square cake pan; line base and sides with baking paper.
3. Beat butter and sugar in small bowl with electric mixer until light and fluffy. Add eggs, one at a time, beating between additions until just combined; transfer to large bowl. Stir in sifted flour and milk, in two batches.
4. Spread mixture into pan; bake 25 minutes.
5. Meanwhile, blend or process ingredients for cinnamon crumble, pulsing until ingredients just come together.
6. Remove cake from oven. Working quickly, toss frozen blackberries in cornflour to coat. Top cake with drained quince then blackberries; sprinkle cinnamon crumble over fruit. Return to oven; bake 20 minutes. Stand cake 5 minutes; turn, top-side up, onto wire rack. Serve cake warm or cold with reserved quince syrup.

POACHED QUINCE Stir the water, sugar, cinnamon stick and juice in medium saucepan over low heat until sugar dissolves. Add quince; bring to a boil. Reduce heat; simmer, covered, about 1 hour 30 minutes or until quince is tender and rosy in colour. Cool quince in syrup to room temperature; strain quince over medium bowl. Reserve quince and syrup separately.

pineapple cake with malibu cream

PREPARATION TIME **25 MINUTES** COOKING TIME **50 MINUTES**

1 cup (75g) shredded coconut
450g can crushed pineapple in syrup
125g butter, softened
½ cup (110g) caster sugar
2 eggs
1½ cups (225g) self-raising flour
6 egg whites
½ cup (110g) caster sugar, extra
2 teaspoons icing sugar

MALIBU CREAM
300ml thickened cream
¼ cup (40g) icing sugar
1 tablespoon Malibu

1. Toast coconut in medium frying pan, stirring constantly, about 2 minutes or until browned lightly. Remove from pan; cool.
2. Drain pineapple over small bowl; reserve ½ cup of the syrup, discard remainder.
3. Preheat oven to moderate (180°C/160°C fan-forced). Grease two deep 20cm-round springform tins; line bases and sides with baking paper.
4. Beat butter and sugar in small bowl with electric mixer until light and fluffy. Add eggs, one at a time, beating until just combined between additions. Transfer mixture to large bowl; stir in sifted flour, pineapple, then reserved syrup. Divide mixture between tins; bake 20 minutes.
5. Meanwhile, beat egg whites in small bowl with electric mixer until soft peaks form; gradually add extra caster sugar, beating until sugar dissolves between additions. Fold in toasted coconut.
6. Remove cakes from oven; working quickly; divide coconut mixture over cakes in tins, using spatula to spread evenly so tops are completely covered. Bake about 30 minutes. Stand cakes in tins 5 minutes; using small knife, carefully loosen meringue from baking paper around inside of tin. Release sides of tins; cool.
7. Meanwhile, beat ingredients for Malibu cream in small bowl with electric mixer until soft peaks form.
8. Place one cake on serving plate; spread with cream. Top with remaining cake; dust with sifted icing sugar.

Cocoa powder is made when chocolate liquor is pressed to remove most of the cocoa butter. The remaining solids are processed to make a fine, unsweetened cocoa powder, which tastes bitter and imparts a deep chocolate flavour to baked items such as brownies, biscuits and some cakes. Used alone in cakes, cocoa powder gives full flavour and dark colour, but it can also be used in recipes with other added chocolate (unsweetened or dark) to produce a cake with a more intense flavour.

family chocolate cake

PREPARATION TIME **20 MINUTES**   COOKING TIME **50 MINUTES (PLUS COOLING TIME)**

2 cups (500ml) water
3 cups (660g) caster sugar
250g butter, chopped
⅓ cup (35g) cocoa powder
1 teaspoon bicarbonate of soda
3 cups (450g) self-raising flour
4 eggs

FUDGE FROSTING
90g butter
⅓ cup (80ml) water
½ cup (110g) caster sugar
1½ cups (240g) icing sugar
⅓ cup (35g) cocoa powder

1. Preheat oven to moderate (180°C/160°C fan-forced). Grease deep 26.5cm x 33cm (14-cup/3.5-litre) baking dish; line base with baking paper.
2. Combine the water, sugar, butter and sifted cocoa and soda in medium saucepan; stir over heat, without boiling, until sugar dissolves. Bring to a boil then reduce heat; simmer, uncovered, 5 minutes. Transfer mixture to large bowl; cool to room temperature.
3. Add flour and eggs to bowl; beat with electric mixer until mixture is smooth and pale in colour. Pour mixture into pan; bake about 50 minutes. Stand cake 10 minutes; turn, top-side up, onto wire rack to cool.
4. Spread cold cake with fudge frosting.

FUDGE FROSTING Combine butter, the water and caster sugar in small saucepan; stir over low heat, without boiling, until sugar dissolves. Sift icing sugar and cocoa into small bowl then gradually stir in hot butter mixture. Cover; refrigerate about 20 minutes or until frosting thickens. Beat with wooden spoon until spreadable.

quick-mix patty cakes

PREPARATION TIME **20 MINUTES** COOKING TIME **20 MINUTES** MAKES **24 PATTY CAKES**

125g butter, softened
½ teaspoon vanilla extract
¾ cup (165g) caster sugar
3 eggs
2 cups (300g) self-raising flour
¼ cup (60ml) milk

1. Preheat oven to moderate (180°C/160°C fan-forced). Line two 12-hole patty pans with paper cases.
2. Combine ingredients in medium bowl; beat with electric mixer on low speed until ingredients are just combined. Increase speed to medium; beat about 3 minutes or until mixture is smooth and paler in colour.
3. Drop rounded tablespoons of mixture into each case; bake about 20 minutes. Stand cakes 5 minutes; turn, top-sides up, onto wire racks to cool.
4. Top cakes with icing of your choice.

VARIATIONS

CHOCOLATE & ORANGE Stir in 1 teaspoon finely grated orange rind and ½ cup (95g) dark Choc Bits at the end of step 2.
PASSIONFRUIT & LIME Stir in 1 teaspoon finely grated lime rind and ¼ cup (60ml) passionfruit pulp at the end of step 2.
BANANA & WHITE CHOCOLATE CHIP Stir in ½ cup overripe mashed banana and ½ cup (95g) white Choc Bits at the end of step 2.
MOCHA Blend 1 tablespoon sifted cocoa powder with 1 tablespoon strong black coffee; stir in at the end of step 2.

glacé icing

2 cups (320g) icing sugar
20g butter, melted
2 tablespoons hot water, approximately

1. Place sifted icing sugar in small bowl; stir in butter and enough of the hot water to make a firm paste; stir over small saucepan of simmering water until spreadable.

VARIATIONS

CHOCOLATE Stir in 1 teaspoon sifted cocoa powder.
COFFEE Dissolve 1 teaspoon instant coffee granules in the hot water.
PASSIONFRUIT Stir in 1 tablespoon passionfruit pulp.

BISCUITS & SLICES

Making a slice or a few trays of sweet biscuits can be fun, is certainly easy and, goodness knows, the end result is a far, far better product than store-bought. Some of our recipes are rich and decadent (perfect with a strong espresso), some simple and homely; others can double as a dessert; and most make a fabulous lunchbox discovery. Don't underestimate the impact these small morsels will create when presented – or how the scent of their baking draws an audience even before they're removed from the oven.

basic vanilla biscuits

PREPARATION TIME **20 MINUTES** BAKING TIME **15 MINUTES** MAKES 30

200g butter, softened
½ teaspoon vanilla extract
1 cup (160g) icing sugar
1 egg
1¾ cups (260g) plain flour
½ teaspoon bicarbonate of soda

1. Preheat oven to moderately slow (170°C/150°C fan-forced). Grease oven trays; line with baking paper.
2. Beat butter, extract, sifted icing sugar and egg in small bowl with electric mixer until light and fluffy. Transfer to medium bowl; stir in sifted flour and soda, in two batches.
3. Roll level tablespoons of dough into balls; place on trays 3cm apart. Bake about 15 minutes; cool biscuits on trays.

VARIATIONS

CRAISIN & COCONUT Stir ½ cup (65g) craisins and ½ cup (40g) shredded coconut into basic biscuit mixture before flour and soda are added.
PEAR & GINGER Stir ¼ cup (35g) finely chopped dried pears, ¼ cup (55g) coarsely chopped glacé ginger and ½ cup (45g) rolled oats into basic biscuit mixture before flour and soda are added.
CHOC CHIP Stir ½ cup (95g) dark Choc Bits into basic biscuit mixture before flour and soda are added. Roll level tablespoons of dough into balls then roll balls in a mixture of 1 tablespoon caster sugar, 2 teaspoons ground nutmeg and 2 teaspoons ground cinnamon.
BROWN SUGAR & PECAN Substitute 1 cup (220g) firmly packed brown sugar for the icing sugar in the basic biscuit mixture. Stir ½ cup (60g) coarsely chopped pecans into basic biscuit mixture before flour and soda are added.

Opposite, clockwise from top left: craisin & coconut; pear & ginger; choc chip; brown sugar & pecan

Walnuts, in addition to being delicious, are the best source by far of all nuts for valuable omega-3 fatty acid content. To chop, either use a large heavy knife or pulse in a food processor. Make sure walnuts are at room temperature before processing and that you don't over-pulse because the nuts will quickly turn into paste rather than the small bits you need for this recipe.

chocolate chip cookies

PREPARATION TIME **15 MINUTES** BAKING TIME **15 MINUTES** MAKES 24

125g butter, softened
½ teaspoon vanilla extract
⅓ cup (75g) caster sugar
⅓ cup (75g) firmly packed brown sugar
1 egg
1 cup (150g) plain flour

½ teaspoon bicarbonate of soda
150g milk eating chocolate,
  chopped coarsely
½ cup (50g) walnuts,
  chopped coarsely

1. Preheat oven to moderate (180°C/160°C fan-forced). Grease oven trays; line with baking paper.
2. Beat butter, extract, sugars and egg in small bowl with electric mixer until smooth; do not overbeat. Transfer mixture to medium bowl; stir in sifted flour and soda then chocolate and nuts.
3. Drop level tablespoons of mixture onto trays 5cm apart. Bake about 15 minutes; cool cookies on trays.

crunchy muesli cookies

PREPARATION TIME **15 MINUTES** COOKING TIME **25 MINUTES** MAKES 36

1 cup (90g) rolled oats
1 cup (150g) plain flour
1 cup (220g) caster sugar
2 teaspoons ground cinnamon
¼ cup (35g) craisins
⅓ cup (55g) finely chopped dried apricots

½ cup (70g) slivered almonds
125g butter
2 tablespoons golden syrup
½ teaspoon bicarbonate of soda
1 tablespoon boiling water

1. Preheat oven to slow (150°C/130°C fan-forced). Grease oven trays; line with baking paper.
2. Combine oats, flour, sugar, cinnamon, dried fruit and nuts in large bowl.
3. Melt butter with golden syrup in small saucepan over low heat; add combined soda and the boiling water. Stir warm butter mixture into dry ingredients.
4. Roll level tablespoons of mixture into balls, place on trays 5cm apart; flatten with hand. Bake about 20 minutes; cool cookies on trays.

If you don't have hazelnut meal in your pantry, it's easy enough to grind the nuts yourself for the small amount required here. Toast the nuts briefly in a small frying pan, stirring constantly to ensure they don't burn. Cool then wrap in a tea-towel and rub off their skins. Process in a coffee- or spice-grinder (or mini food processor) to a coarse meal consistency. Take care – too long and they'll turn into an oily paste.

hazelnut pinwheels

PREPARATION TIME **20 MINUTES (PLUS REFRIGERATION TIME)** BAKING TIME **20 MINUTES** MAKES 30

1¼ cups (185g) plain flour
100g butter, chopped
½ cup (110g) caster sugar
1 egg yolk
1 tablespoon milk, approximately
⅓ cup (110g) chocolate hazelnut spread
2 tablespoons hazelnut meal

1. Preheat oven to moderate (180°C/160°C fan-forced). Grease oven trays; line with baking paper.
2. Process flour, butter and sugar until crumbly. Add egg yolk; process with enough milk until mixture forms a ball. Knead dough on lightly floured surface until smooth; cover, refrigerate 1 hour.
3. Roll dough between sheets of baking paper to form 20cm x 30cm rectangle; remove top sheet of paper. Spread dough evenly with hazelnut spread; sprinkle with hazelnut meal. Using paper as a guide, roll dough tightly from long side to enclose filling. Enclose roll in plastic wrap; refrigerate 30 minutes.
4. Remove plastic; cut roll into 1cm slices. Place slices on trays 2cm apart. Bake about 20 minutes. Stand pinwheels on trays 5 minutes; transfer to wire rack to cool.

frangipane jam drops

PREPARATION TIME **30 MINUTES** BAKING TIME **15 MINUTES** MAKES 24

125g butter, softened
½ teaspoon vanilla extract
½ cup (110g) caster sugar
1 cup (120g) almond meal
1 egg
⅔ cup (100g) plain flour
2 tablespoons raspberry jam

1. Preheat oven to moderate (180°C/160°C fan forced). Grease oven trays; line with baking paper.
2. Beat butter, extract, sugar and almond meal in small bowl with electric mixer until light and fluffy. Add egg, beating until just combined; stir in sifted flour.
3. Drop level tablespoons of mixture on trays 5cm apart. Use handle of wooden spoon to make small hole (about 1cm deep) in top of each biscuit; fill each hole with ¼ teaspoon jam. Bake about 15 minutes; cool jam drops on trays.

vanilla bean thins

PREPARATION TIME **20 MINUTES** BAKING TIME **5 MINUTES** MAKES 24

1 vanilla bean
30g butter, softened
¼ cup (55g) caster sugar
1 egg white, beaten lightly
¼ cup (35g) plain flour

1. Preheat oven to moderately hot (200°C/180°C fan-forced). Grease oven trays; line with baking paper.
2. Halve vanilla bean lengthways; scrape seeds into medium bowl with butter and sugar, discard vanilla pod. Stir until combined, stir in egg white and flour. Spoon mixture into piping bag fitted with 5mm plain tube.
3. Pipe 6cm-long strips (making them slightly wider at both ends) 5cm apart on trays. Bake about 5 minutes or until edges are browned lightly; cool biscuits on trays.

golden pecan twists

PREPARATION TIME **25 MINUTES** BAKING TIME **10 MINUTES** MAKES 30

2 tablespoons golden syrup
⅓ cup (40g) finely chopped pecans
125g butter, softened
¼ teaspoon vanilla extract
⅓ cup (75g) caster sugar
1 egg yolk
1 cup (150g) plain flour

1. Preheat oven to moderate (180°C/160°C fan-forced). Grease oven trays; line with baking paper.
2. Combine half of the golden syrup with nuts in small bowl.
3. Beat butter, extract, sugar, remaining golden syrup and egg yolk in small bowl with electric mixer until light and fluffy. Stir in sifted flour.
4. Shape rounded teaspoons of mixture into balls; roll each ball into 12cm log. Twist each log into a loop, overlapping one end over the other. Place twists on trays 3cm apart; top each twist with ½ teaspoon nut mixture. Bake about 10 minutes; cool twists on trays.

coffee almond biscuits

PREPARATION TIME **15 MINUTES** BAKING TIME **15 MINUTES** MAKES 24

1 tablespoon instant coffee granules
3 teaspoons hot water
3 cups (360g) almond meal
1 cup (220g) caster sugar
2 tablespoons coffee-flavoured liqueur
3 egg whites, beaten lightly
24 coffee beans

1. Preheat oven to moderate (180°C/160°C fan-forced). Grease oven trays; line with baking paper.
2. Dissolve coffee in the hot water in large bowl. Add almond meal, sugar, liqueur and egg whites; stir until mixture forms a firm paste.
3. Roll level tablespoons of mixture into balls; place on trays 3cm apart; flatten with hand. Press coffee beans into tops of biscuits. Bake about 15 minutes; cool biscuits on trays.

Finely chopped walnuts, hazelnuts or macadamias can be used instead of pecans in the twists if you prefer. Consider using chocolate-covered coffee beans for the coffee almond biscuit tops, or even an almond kernel.

These biscuits are a scrumptious way to consume a bit of healthy fibre. Unprocessed bran is the coarse outer husk of cereal grains, and can be found in health food stores and supermarkets. Use traditional rolled oats for this recipe, not the instant variety.

oat and bran biscuits

PREPARATION TIME **15 MINUTES (PLUS REFRIGERATION TIME)** BAKING TIME **15 MINUTES** MAKES 30

1 cup (150g) plain flour
1 cup (60g) unprocessed bran
¾ cup (60g) rolled oats
½ teaspoon bicarbonate of soda

60g butter, chopped
½ cup (110g) caster sugar
1 egg
2 tablespoons water, approximately

1. Process flour, bran, oats, soda and butter until crumbly; add sugar, egg and enough of the water to make a firm dough. Knead dough on lightly floured surface until smooth; cover, refrigerate 30 minutes.

2. Preheat oven to moderate (180°C/160°C fan-forced). Grease oven trays; line with baking paper.

3. Divide dough in half; roll each half between sheets of baking paper to about 5mm thickness. Cut dough into 7cm rounds; place on trays 2cm apart. Bake about 15 minutes. Stand biscuits on trays 5 minutes; transfer to wire rack to cool.

chocolate lace crisps

PREPARATION TIME **25 MINUTES (PLUS REFRIGERATION TIME)** COOKING TIME **20 MINUTES** MAKES 24

100g dark cooking chocolate,
  chopped coarsely
80g butter, chopped
1 cup (220g) caster sugar
1 egg, beaten lightly

1 cup (150g) plain flour
2 tablespoons cocoa powder
¼ teaspoon bicarbonate of soda
¼ cup (40g) icing sugar

1. Melt chocolate and butter in small saucepan over low heat. Transfer to medium bowl.
2. Stir in caster sugar, egg and sifted flour, cocoa and soda. Cover; refrigerate about 15 minutes or until mixture is firm enough to handle.
3. Preheat oven to moderate (180°C/160°C fan-forced). Grease oven trays; line with baking paper.
4. Roll level tablespoons of mixture into balls; roll each ball in icing sugar, place on trays 8cm apart. Bake about 15 minutes; cool crisps on trays.

maple-syrup butter cookies

PREPARATION TIME **20 MINUTES** BAKING TIME **15 MINUTES** MAKES 24

125g butter, softened
½ teaspoon vanilla extract
⅓ cup (80ml) maple syrup
¾ cup (110g) plain flour
¼ cup (35g) cornflour

1. Preheat oven to moderate (180°C/160°C fan-forced). Grease oven trays; line with baking paper.
2. Beat butter, extract and maple syrup in small bowl with electric mixer until light and fluffy; stir in combined sifted flours. Spoon mixture into piping bag fitted with 1cm fluted tube.
3. Pipe stars about 3cm apart onto trays. Bake about 15 minutes; cool cookies on trays.

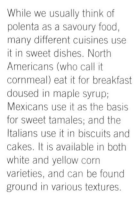

While we usually think of polenta as a savoury food, many different cuisines use it in sweet dishes. North Americans (who call it cornmeal) eat it for breakfast doused in maple syrup; Mexicans use it as the basis for sweet tamales; and the Italians use it in biscuits and cakes. It is available in both white and yellow corn varieties, and can be found ground in various textures.

polenta and orange biscuits

PREPARATION TIME **15 MINUTES** BAKING TIME **15 MINUTES** MAKES 30

125g butter, softened
2 teaspoons finely grated orange rind
⅔ cup (110g) icing sugar
⅓ cup (55g) polenta
1 cup (150g) plain flour

1. Preheat oven to moderate (180°C/160°C fan-forced). Grease oven trays; line with baking paper.
2. Beat butter, rind and sifted icing sugar in small bowl with electric mixer until just combined; stir in polenta and sifted flour. Shape mixture into 30cm-rectangular log; cut log into 1cm slices.
3. Place slices on trays 2cm apart. Bake about 15 minutes. Stand biscuits on trays 5 minutes; transfer to wire rack to cool.

coffee hazelnut meringues

PREPARATION TIME **10 MINUTES (PLUS COOLING TIME)** BAKING TIME **45 MINUTES** MAKES 30

2 egg whites
½ cup (110g) caster sugar
2 teaspoons instant coffee granules
½ teaspoon hot water
3 teaspoons coffee-flavoured liqueur
¼ cup (35g) roasted hazelnuts

1. Preheat oven to very slow (120°C/100°C fan-forced). Grease oven trays; line with baking paper.
2. Beat egg whites in small bowl with electric mixer until soft peaks form. Gradually add sugar, beating until dissolved between additions.
3. Meanwhile, dissolve coffee in the water in small jug; stir in liqueur. Fold coffee mixture into meringue mixture.
4. Spoon mixture into piping bag fitted with 5mm fluted tube. Pipe meringues onto trays 2cm apart; top each meringue with a nut.
5. Bake about 45 minutes. Cool meringues in oven with door ajar.

choc-peppermint slice

PREPARATION TIME **10 MINUTES (PLUS REFRIGERATION TIME)** COOKING TIME **10 MINUTES** MAKES 24

250g plain sweet biscuits
100g butter, chopped
½ cup (125ml) sweetened condensed milk
2 x 35g Peppermint Crisp chocolate bars, chopped coarsely

CHOCOLATE TOPPING
200g milk eating chocolate, chopped coarsely
2 teaspoons vegetable oil

1. Grease 19cm x 29cm slice pan; line base and two long sides with baking paper, extending paper 2cm over long sides.
2. Process 200g of the biscuits until fine. Chop remaining biscuits coarsely.
3. Combine butter and milk in small saucepan; stir over low heat until smooth. Combine processed and chopped biscuits with chocolate bar in medium bowl; stir in butter mixture. Press mixture firmly into pan; refrigerate, covered, about 20 minutes or until set.
4. Meanwhile, stir ingredients for chocolate topping in small heatproof bowl over small saucepan of simmering water, until smooth; spread mixture over slice. Refrigerate until firm before cutting into 24 squares.

VARIATIONS
LEMON Replace Peppermint Crisp bars with 1 teaspoon finely grated lemon rind and 1 tablespoon lemon juice in the biscuit mixture. Press mixture firmly into pan; refrigerate, covered, about 20 minutes or until set. Top with lemon icing made by stirring 1¼ cups (200g) icing sugar with 10g butter and one tablespoon lemon juice in small heatproof bowl over small saucepan of simmering water until smooth.
APRICOT & COCONUT Replace Peppermint Crisp bars with ½ cup (40g) toasted shredded coconut and ½ cup (80g) finely chopped dried apricots in the biscuit mixture. Press mixture firmly into pan; refrigerate, covered, about 20 minutes or until set. Top with icing made by stirring 200g coarsely chopped white eating chocolate and 2 teaspoons vegetable oil in small heatproof bowl over small saucepan of simmering water until smooth.
COFFEE & MACADAMIA Replace Peppermint Crisp bars with ½ cup (70g) coarsely chopped roasted macadamias in the biscuit mixture. Press mixture firmly into pan; refrigerate, covered, about 20 minutes or until set. Top with icing made by dissolving 2 teaspoons instant coffee granules in 2 tablespoons boiling water in small heatproof bowl over small saucepan of simmering water; add 1¼ cups (200g) icing sugar and 10g butter, stirring until smooth.

Opposite, clockwise from top left: choc-peppermint slice; lemon slice; apricot & coconut slice; coffee & macadamia slice

Always use a premium-quality eating chocolate when baking rather than compound or any labelled light or low fat. The important thing is to use "real" chocolate, which means that it has to contain cocoa butter. If cocoa butter isn't shown on the packaging, don't buy it.

berry sponge slice

PREPARATION TIME **20 MINUTES** BAKING TIME **30 MINUTES** MAKES 20

2 sheets ready-rolled sweet
  puff pastry, thawed
3 eggs
½ cup (110g) caster sugar
½ cup (75g) self-raising flour

1½ cups (225g) frozen mixed berries
1 egg white, beaten lightly
1 tablespoon caster sugar, extra
1 tablespoon icing sugar

1. Preheat oven to hot (220°C/200°C fan-forced). Grease 25cm x 30cm swiss roll pan.
2. Roll one pastry sheet until large enough to cover base of pan, extending pastry halfway up sides. Prick pastry with fork at 2cm intervals; freeze 5 minutes.
3. Place another swiss roll pan on top of pastry; bake 5 minutes. Remove top pan; bake further 5 minutes or until pastry is browned lightly. Cool 5 minutes.
4. Meanwhile, beat eggs and sugar in small bowl with electric mixer until thick and creamy; fold in sifted flour. Spread mixture evenly over pastry; sprinkle evenly with berries.
5. Roll remaining pastry sheet large enough to fit pan; place over berries. Brush pastry with egg white, sprinkle with extra sugar; score pastry in crosshatch pattern.
6. Bake about 20 minutes. Cool in pan; dust with sifted icing sugar then cut into squares.

choc-peanut caramel slice

PREPARATION TIME **20 MINUTES (PLUS COOLING AND REFRIGERATION TIME)** COOKING TIME **20 MINUTES** MAKES 40

125g butter, chopped
1 cup (220g) caster sugar
395g can sweetened condensed milk
1 cup (140g) roasted unsalted peanuts
200g dark eating chocolate
20g butter, extra

1. Grease deep 19cm-square cake pan. Fold 40cm piece of foil lengthways into thirds; place foil strip over base and up two sides of pan (this will help lift the slice out of the pan). Line base with baking paper.
2. Combine butter, sugar and milk in medium heavy-based saucepan; stir over medium heat, without boiling, until sugar dissolves. Bring to a boil; boil, stirring constantly, about 10 minutes or until caramel mixture becomes a dark-honey colour and starts to come away from the base and side of pan.
3. Working quickly and carefully (the mixture is very hot), pour caramel into pan; smooth with metal spatula. Press nuts into caramel with spatula; cool 20 minutes.
4. Stir chocolate and extra butter in small heatproof bowl over small saucepan of simmering water until smooth; spread chocolate mixture over slice. Refrigerate until set. Use foil strip to lift slice from pan before cutting into squares.

Use dry, grease-free utensils to beat room temperature egg whites, watching carefully for the forming of "soft" peaks, those that literally fall over when the beaters are lifted. Beating the mixture any longer is likely to make it so dry that the sugar won't dissolve.

lemon meringue slice

PREPARATION TIME **20 MINUTES** BAKING TIME **1 HOUR (PLUS COOLING TIME)** MAKES 16

90g butter, softened
2 tablespoons caster sugar
1 egg
1 cup (150g) plain flour
¼ cup (80g) apricot jam

LEMON TOPPING
2 eggs
2 egg yolks
½ cup (110g) caster sugar
300ml cream
1 tablespoon finely grated lemon rind
2 tablespoons lemon juice

MERINGUE
3 egg whites
¾ cup (165g) caster sugar

1. Preheat oven to moderately hot (200°C/180°C fan-forced). Grease base of 19cm x 29cm slice pan; line base and two long sides with baking paper, extending paper 2cm over long sides.

2. Beat butter, sugar and egg in small bowl with electric mixer until pale in colour; stir in sifted flour, in two batches. Press dough over base of pan; prick several times with fork. Bake about 15 minutes or until browned lightly. Cool 20 minutes; spread base with jam.

3. Reduce oven temperature to moderately slow (170°C/150°C fan-forced).

4. Place lemon topping ingredients in medium bowl; whisk until combined. Pour lemon topping over base. Bake about 35 minutes or until set; cool 20 minutes. Roughen surface of topping with fork.

5. Increase oven temperature to hot (220°C/200°C fan-forced).

6. To make meringue, beat egg whites in small bowl with electric mixer until soft peaks form; gradually add sugar, beating until dissolved between additions.

7. Spread meringue evenly over topping; bake about 3 minutes or until browned lightly. Cool in pan 20 minutes before cutting.

Glacé ginger is fresh ginger root preserved in a sugar syrup; it has a smooth, rich ginger flavour with an added hint of subtle heat. It can be eaten as a snack as well as (by far its most common use) used to add a flavourful burst of ginger when baking. Crystallised ginger can be substituted if rinsed with warm water and dried before using.

apple and prune slice

PREPARATION TIME **20 MINUTES** COOKING TIME **1 HOUR 10 MINUTES (PLUS COOLING TIME)** MAKES 24

4 medium apples (600g)
¾ cup (135g) coarsely chopped
  seeded prunes
2½ cups (625ml) water
½ teaspoon ground cinnamon

½ teaspoon ground nutmeg
2 tablespoons hazelnut meal
2 sheets ready-rolled shortcrust
  pastry, thawed
1 tablespoon caster sugar

1. Peel and core apples; slice thinly. Place apples and prunes in medium saucepan with the water, bring to a boil. Reduce heat, simmer, covered, 10 minutes or until apples are just tender. Drain well; cool 15 minutes.
2. Combine cinnamon, nutmeg and hazelnut meal in medium bowl; gently stir in apple mixture.
3. Preheat oven to moderately hot (200°C/180°C fan-forced). Grease 20cm x 30cm lamington pan; line base with baking paper.
4. Roll one pastry sheet large enough to cover base of pan; place in pan, trim edges. Cover pastry with baking paper, fill with dried beans or rice; bake 15 minutes. Remove paper and beans; bake 5 minutes. Spread apple mixture over pastry.
5. Roll remaining pastry sheet large enough to fit pan; place over apple filling. Brush pastry with a little water, sprinkle with sugar; score pastry in crosshatch pattern. Bake about 45 minutes. Cool in pan; cut into squares.

dutch ginger and almond slice

PREPARATION TIME **15 MINUTES** BAKING TIME **35 MINUTES** MAKES 20

1¾ cups (255g) plain flour
1 cup (220g) caster sugar
⅔ cup (150g) coarsely chopped
  glacé ginger
½ cup (80g) blanched almonds,
  chopped coarsely

1 egg
185g butter, melted
2 teaspoons icing sugar

1. Preheat oven to moderate (180°C/160°C fan-forced). Line 20cm x 30cm lamington pan with baking paper, extending paper 2cm over long sides.
2. Combine flour, sugar, ginger, nuts and egg in medium bowl; stir in butter.
3. Press mixture into pan; bake about 35 minutes. Stand slice in pan 10 minutes before lifting onto wire rack to cool. Dust with sifted icing sugar before cutting.

chocolate hazelnut slice

PREPARATION TIME **30 MINUTES** BAKING TIME **40 MINUTES (PLUS COOLING AND REFRIGERATION TIME)** MAKES 24

250g plain chocolate biscuits
60g butter, melted
4 eggs, separated
¾ cup (165g) caster sugar
½ cup (50g) hazelnut meal
2 tablespoons plain flour

TOPPING
125g butter, softened
½ cup (110g) caster sugar
1 tablespoon orange juice
200g dark eating chocolate, melted
1 tablespoon cocoa powder

1. Preheat oven to moderate (180°C/160°C fan-forced). Grease 20cm x 30cm lamington pan; line base and two long sides with baking paper, extending paper 2cm over long sides.

2. Process biscuits until fine. Combine one cup of the biscuit crumbs with butter in medium bowl; press over base of pan. Refrigerate 10 minutes.

3. Beat egg whites in small bowl with electric mixer until soft peaks form. Gradually add sugar, beating until dissolved between additions; fold in hazelnut meal, remaining biscuit crumbs and flour.

4. Spread egg white mixture over biscuit base; bake 20 minutes. Cool 20 minutes. Reduce oven to moderately slow (170°C/150°C fan-forced).

5. Meanwhile, make topping by beating butter, sugar, egg yolks and juice in small bowl with electric mixer until light and fluffy. Stir in cooled chocolate.

6. Spread topping over slice; bake about 20 minutes, cool in pan. Refrigerate until firm; dust with sifted cocoa before cutting.

turkish delight rocky road

PREPARATION TIME **15 MINUTES** COOKING TIME **5 MINUTES (PLUS REFRIGERATION TIME)** MAKES 28

400g white eating chocolate, chopped coarsely
200g raspberry and vanilla marshmallows, chopped coarsely
200g turkish delight, chopped finely
¾ cup (110g) toasted macadamias, chopped coarsely

1. Line two 8cm x 25cm bar pans with baking paper, extending paper 2cm over all sides of pans.

2. Stir chocolate in medium heatproof bowl over medium saucepan of simmering water until smooth; cool 2 minutes.

3. Meanwhile, combine remaining ingredients in large bowl. Working quickly, stir in chocolate; spread mixture into pans. Refrigerate until set; cut into 1cm slices.

Turkish delight, also known as lokum, is a sweet made of a flavouring (traditionally rose, vanilla, pistachio or orange), sugar syrup, nuts and dried fruit bound together with mastic (gum arabic). According to legend, turkish delight was developed by one of the Ottoman sultans to appeal to the hundreds of women in his harem. The recipe, virtually unchanged for the past 500 years, proved an overwhelming success and this unique confectionery has become a sweet revered around the world.

Baklava, eaten in one form or another by millions of people around the world, is not at all difficult to make at home. Here's a clever idea for another way to eat it: crush then crumble a few pieces of baklava into some softened good-quality vanilla ice-cream; stir to combine then re-freeze until quite firm. Serve sliced baklava ice-cream at the end of a summer's night dinner for a treat.

rosewater baklava

PREPARATION TIME **15 MINUTES** COOKING TIME **35 MINUTES** MAKES 16

1 cup (160g) blanched almonds
1 cup (140g) shelled pistachios
2 teaspoons ground cinnamon
1 teaspoon ground clove
1 teaspoon ground nutmeg
18 sheets fillo pastry
80g butter, melted

ROSEWATER SYRUP
1 cup (250ml) water
1 cup (220g) caster sugar
¼ cup (90g) honey
1 teaspoon rosewater

1. Preheat oven to moderate (180°C/160°C fan-forced). Grease deep 23cm-square cake pan.

2. Process nuts and spices until chopped finely; spread nut mixture onto oven tray. Roast, uncovered, about 10 minutes or until browned lightly.

3. Increase oven temperature to moderately hot (200°C/180°C fan-forced).

4. Cut pastry sheets to fit base of pan; layer three pastry squares, brushing each with butter; place in pan, sprinkle with ⅓ cup of the nut mixture. Repeat layering with remaining pastry, butter and nut mixture, ending with pastry.

5. Using sharp knife, cut baklava into quarters; cut each quarter in half on the diagonal, then cut each triangle in half. Bake 25 minutes.

6. Reduce heat to slow (150°C/130°C fan-forced), bake baklava further 10 minutes.

7. Meanwhile, combine ingredients for rosewater syrup in small saucepan. Stir over heat, without boiling, until sugar dissolves; bring to a boil then simmer, uncovered, without stirring, about 5 minutes or until thickened slightly.

8. Pour hot syrup over hot baklava; cool in pan.

craisin and pistachio muesli slice

PREPARATION TIME **20 MINUTES** COOKING TIME **20 MINUTES** MAKES 30

125g butter
⅓ cup (75g) firmly packed brown sugar
2 tablespoons honey
1½ cups (135g) rolled oats

½ cup (75g) self-raising flour
1 cup (130g) craisins
1 cup (140g) toasted shelled pistachios,
  chopped coarsely

1. Preheat oven to moderate (180°C/160°C fan-forced). Grease 20cm x 30cm lamington pan; line base and two long sides with baking paper, extending paper 2cm above long sides.
2. Melt butter with sugar and honey in medium saucepan over medium heat without boiling, stirring, until sugar is dissolved.
3. Stir remaining ingredients into butter mixture.
4. Press mixture firmly into pan; bake about 20 minutes. Cool in pan before cutting.

rum and raisin chocolate slice

PREPARATION TIME **20 MINUTES (PLUS STANDING AND REFRIGERATION TIME)** COOKING TIME **15 MINUTES** MAKES 12

½ cup (75g) coarsely chopped raisins
2 tablespoons dark rum, warmed
150g milk eating chocolate, chopped coarsely
2 teaspoons vegetable oil
¼ cup (60ml) cream
200g dark eating chocolate, chopped coarsely

1. Combine raisins and rum in small bowl. Cover; stand 3 hours or overnight.
2. Grease 8cm x 25cm bar cake pan; line base and two long sides with foil, extending foil 5cm over long sides.
3. Stir half of the milk chocolate and half of the oil in small heatproof bowl over small saucepan of simmering water until smooth; spread mixture over base of pan. Refrigerate about 10 minutes or until set.
4. Combine cream and dark chocolate in small saucepan; stir over low heat until smooth. Stir in raisin mixture, spread over chocolate base; refrigerate 20 minutes or until set.
5. Stir remaining milk chocolate and oil in small heatproof bowl over small saucepan of simmering water until smooth; spread over raisin mixture. Refrigerate about 40 minutes or until set; remove from pan before cutting.

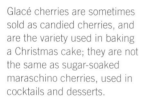

Glacé cherries are sometimes sold as candied cherries, and are the variety used in baking a Christmas cake; they are not the same as sugar-soaked maraschino cherries, used in cocktails and desserts.

choc-cherry macaroon slice

PREPARATION TIME 15 MINUTES   BAKING TIME 45 MINUTES (PLUS COOLING AND REFRIGERATION TIME)   MAKES 16

3 egg whites
½ cup (110g) caster sugar
100g dark eating chocolate,
  grated coarsely
¼ cup (35g) plain flour

1⅓ cups (95g) shredded
  coconut, toasted
¾ cup (150g) glacé cherries,
  chopped coarsely
50g dark eating chocolate, melted

1. Preheat oven to slow (150°C/130°C fan-forced). Grease base of 19cm x 29cm slice pan; line base and two long sides with baking paper, extending paper 2cm over long sides.
2. Beat egg whites in small bowl with electric mixer until soft peaks form; gradually add sugar, beating until dissolved between additions.
3. Fold in grated chocolate, flour, coconut and cherries.
4. Spread mixture into pan; bake about 45 minutes. Cool to room temperature in pan.
5. Drizzle slice with melted chocolate; refrigerate until set before cutting.

cherry friand slice

PREPARATION TIME 15 MINUTES   BAKING TIME 40 MINUTES   MAKES 16

4 egg whites
100g butter, melted
1 tablespoon milk
½ teaspoon vanilla extract
1 cup (125g) almond meal

1 cup (160g) icing sugar
⅓ cup (50g) self-raising flour
1 vanilla bean
⅔ cup (100g) frozen cherries,
  chopped coarsely

1. Preheat oven to moderately slow (170°C/150°C fan-forced). Grease 19cm x 29cm slice pan; line base and two long sides with baking paper, extending paper 5cm over long sides.
2. Place egg whites in large bowl, whisk with fork until combined. Add butter, milk, extract, almond meal and sifted icing sugar and flour; stir until just combined. Split vanilla bean in half lengthways; scrape seeds from bean, stir seeds into mixture.
3. Pour mixture into pan; sprinkle cherries over mixture. Bake about 30 minutes; stand in pan 10 minutes before lifting slice onto wire rack to cool. Dust with sifted icing sugar, if desired.

BAKING BASICS

How to best use your oven

There are many different types of ovens and energy sources, so it's important that you get to know your oven – particularly when it comes to baking cakes, biscuits and slices. The recipes in this book were tested in domestic-sized electric fan-forced ovens.

If you are using a fan-forced oven, check the operating instructions for best results. As a rule, reduce the temperature by 10°C to 20°C when using the fan during baking (we indicate this in each recipe); recipes might also take slightly less time to bake than specified. Some ovens give better results if the fan is used for only part of the baking time; in this case, it is usually best to introduce the fan about halfway through the baking time.

We positioned the oven racks and pan(s) so that the top of the baked cake, tray of biscuits or slices will be roughly in the centre of the oven.

Best results are obtained by baking in an oven preheated to the desired temperature; this takes at least 10 minutes.

How to prepare a cake pan

We prefer to use aluminium pans for baking whenever possible. Be aware that cake pans made from materials with various coatings such as non-stick and the newer high-temperature silicone, work well provided the surface is unscratched. Pans made from tin and stainless steel do not conduct heat as evenly as does aluminium. If using these pans, reduce the oven temperature by 10°C.

To grease a cake pan, use either a light, even coating of cooking-oil spray, or a pastry brush to brush melted butter evenly over the base and side(s).

Cakes that are high in sugar, or that contain golden syrup, treacle or honey, have a tendency to stick so we recommend lining the base and/or side(s) of the pans. We have indicated in the recipes when this is necessary.

Trace around the base of the pan with a pencil onto greaseproof or baking paper; cut out the shape, slightly inside the pencil mark, so that the paper fits snugly inside the greased pan. In most cases, it is

To line the side of a cake pan, make short diagonal cuts, about 2cm apart, in the lining paper; fit the cut section around the curve (or corners) of the base of the pan.

CAKE-MAKING TIPS

• Use an electric beater to mix cakes, and always have the ingredients at room temperature, particularly the butter. Melted or extremely soft butter will alter the texture of the baked cake.

• Start mixing ingredients on a low speed; once the mixture is combined, increase the speed to about medium and beat for the required time.

• Creamed mixtures for cakes can be mixed with a wooden spoon, but this takes longer.

• When measuring liquids, always stand the marked measuring jug on a flat surface and check at eye level for accuracy.

• Spoon measurements should be levelled off with a knife or spatula.

Biscuits

OVEN TRAYS

We use aluminium oven trays with no or very shallow sides so the heat can circulate freely around the biscuits. The recipe will indicate whether or not to grease or line trays. It's important not to over-grease trays as this can cause biscuits to burn on the bottom.

OVEN POSITION

Two or more trays of biscuits can be baked at the same time; leave a 2cm space around trays to allow for proper heat circulation and browning. During baking time, swap and rotate the trays to ensure even browning.

MIXING

For best results, have all ingredients at room temperature. Do not overbeat butter and sugar as this can result in a soft mixture causing biscuits to spread too much during baking.

TESTING BISCUITS

Baking times in this book are a guide only. Biscuits generally feel soft in the oven and become firmer when cold. To test if biscuits are cooked, push one gently; if it moves on the oven tray without breaking, it is cooked.

STORING BISCUITS

To prevent biscuits from softening, cool them completely before storing. Keep biscuits in an airtight container just large enough to hold them. To freeze un-iced or unfilled biscuits, place cooled biscuits in an airtight container, using sheets of baking paper between layers.

not necessary to grease baking paper once it is in position.

If the recipe indicates that the side(s) of a pan needs to be lined, do so with a baking paper "collar", extending it about 5cm above the edge of the pan, to protect the top of the cake. Fruit cake needs more than a single layer of paper to prevent the cake drying out during the longer baking time. Our method of lining round or square cake pans allows for this, using baking or greaseproof paper:

• For side(s), cut three paper strips long enough to fit around inside of the pan and 8cm wider than the depth of the pan. Fold strips lengthways about 2cm from the edge and make short diagonal cuts about 2cm apart, up to the fold. This helps ease the paper around the curve or corners of the pan, with cut section fitting around the base [see page 113].

• Using the base of the pan as a guide, cut three paper circles (or squares) as instructed previously; position over the base of the pan after lining sides.

To test if a cake is cooked

All cake baking times are approximate. Check cake just after suggested baking time; it should be brown and starting to shrink from the side(s) of the pan. Feel the top with your fingertips; it should feel firm. You may want to insert a thin skewer into the deepest part of the cake from top to base (we prefer to use a metal skewer rather than wooden as any mixture adhering to it is easier to see). As the skewer is removed gently, it should have no uncooked mixture clinging to it. Do not confuse mixture with stickiness from fruit.

Cooling a cake

We have suggested standing a cake for up to 15 minutes before turning it onto a wire rack to cool further. The best way to do this, after standing time has elapsed, is to hold the cake pan firmly and shake it gently; this helps loosen the cake in the pan. Turn the cake, upside-down, onto a wire rack then turn the cake top-side up immediately using a second rack (unless directed otherwise). Some wire racks can mark a cake, particularly a soft one such as a sponge. To prevent this, cover the rack with baking paper.

We have indicated when it is best to cool a cake in the pan; it is always covered with foil before cooling, and will usually be a fruit cake.

How to keep a cake

Most cakes will keep well for two or three days depending on the climate and type of cake; as a rule, remember that the higher the fat content, the longer a cake keeps.

• Cool the cake to room temperature before storing it in an airtight container as close in size to the cake as possible to minimise the amount of air around the cake.

• For a cake that is suitable to freeze, it is usually better to do so unfilled and un-iced because icing can crack during the thawing process. A cake thaws best overnight in the refrigerator. Wrap or seal the cake in freezer wrap or freezer bags, expelling as much air as possible.

• We prefer to store a rich fruit cake in the refrigerator simply because it will cut better; once sliced, it quickly returns to room temperature.

---

1. deep 19cm-square cake pan **2.** deep 23cm-square cake pan **3.** 25cm x 30cm swiss roll pan **4.** 20cm-round sandwich pan **5.** patty pan **6.** 14cm x 21cm loaf pan **7.** 19cm x 29cm slice pan **8.** 24cm bundt pan **9.** deep 22cm-round cake pan

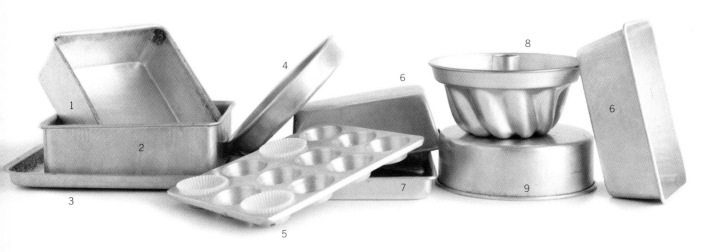

My butter cake wasn't perfect...

Sinks in centre after baking
This generally means that the cake is undercooked.

Sinks in centre while still baking
Mixture is forced to rise too quickly because the oven is too hot.

Sugary crust
Butter and sugar have probably not been creamed sufficiently. Excess sugar was used.

White specks on top
Sugar has not been dissolved enough. It is best to use caster sugar, which dissolves easily during baking. Mixture not creamed sufficiently.

Excessive shrinking
Cake baked at too high a temperature for too long.

Crumbles when cut
Mixture may have been creamed too much, particularly in fruit cakes.

Sticks to pan
Too much sugar or other sweetening in recipe. If a recipe contains honey or golden syrup, or if you're using a new pan, it is wise to line the evenly greased pan with baking paper.

Rises and cracks in centre
Caused by using a cake pan that is too small; most cakes baked in loaf, bar or ring pans crack slightly due to the confined space of the pan. Oven may have been too hot.

Collar around top outside edge
Cake was probably baked at too high a temperature.

Pale on top
This is caused by using a too-large pan or having the lining paper too high around sides of pan.

Coloured streaks on top
Ingredients have not been mixed together enough. Bowl scrapings have not been mixed thoroughly into cake mixture.

Uneven rising
Oven shelf has not been set straight or oven not level on the floor. Mixture not spread evenly into pan.

Holes in baked cake
Occurs if mixture not creamed sufficiently. Oven is too hot.

My fruit cake wasn't perfect...

Fruit sinks to bottom
Fruit not dried thoroughly after washing. Cake mixture too soft to support weight of the fruit (caused by over-creaming). Fruit should be finely chopped to about the size of a sultana so mixture can support it. Self-raising flour may have been used instead of plain flour.

Doughy in centre
Cake baked in too cool an oven, or for not long enough.

Burnt bottom
Cake wrongly positioned in oven or pans lined incorrectly. Cake baked at too high a temperature. Rich fruit cakes require protection during long, slow baking times. Cakes that are 22cm or smaller require three thicknesses of baking-paper lining; larger cakes need one or two sheets of brown paper and three sheets of baking paper.

Cracks on top
Oven at too high a temperature.

Uneven rising
Oven shelf or oven not level. Mixture spread unevenly in pan; use a wet spatula to level top of cake mixture.

Creamed mixture curdles
Eggs and butter not at room temperature. Eggs not added quickly enough to creamed butter and sugar mixture. Eggs used are too large for mixture to absorb the excess liquid. If eggs used are larger than 60g in weight, omit one of the number shown in ingredients list, or add only the yolk of one of the eggs. Curdled creamed mixture could cause finished cake to crumble when cut.

Sinks in the middle
Self-raising flour used, or too much bicarbonate of soda. (Usually only plain flour is used in rich fruit cake, but sometimes a small portion of self-raising flour is added.)
Cake may not have been baked properly. To test, push sharp-pointed knife, rather than a skewer, through centre to base of pan; blade surface helps distinguish between uncooked mixture or fruit and cooked mixture. Test only after minimum specified baking time.

My sponge cake wasn't perfect...

Small white specks on top
Caused by undissolved sugar; sugar should be added gradually to beaten eggs and beaten until completely dissolved between additions.

Shrinks in oven
Cake baked at too high a temperature or for too long.

Wrinkles during cooling
Insufficient baking time. Cake cooled in a draughty area.

Flat and tough
Incorrect folding in of flour and liquid. Triple-sifted flour should be folded into mixture in a gentle, circular motion.

Pale and sticky on top
Baking at too low an oven temperature, or wrong oven position.

Crusty
Baking at too high an oven temperature, wrong oven position or pan too small. Using high-sided cake pans protects the cake mixture.

Sinks in centre
Pan too small, causing cake to rise quickly, then fall in the centre.

Streaks on top
Scrapings from mixing bowl not mixed into sponge mixture; scrapings are always slightly darker than the rest of the mixture. It is best to put scrapings from the mixing bowl towards the side of the pan – not in the centre.

Sponge rises too quickly
Oven temperature may be too high.

Sponge is undercooked
Oven door may have been opened during first half of baking.

GLOSSARY

ALLSPICE also known as pimento or jamaican pepper; tastes like a combination of clove, nutmeg, cumin and cinnamon.

ALMOND flat, pointy-ended nuts with pitted brown shell enclosing a creamy white kernel that is covered by a brown skin.
blanched skins removed.
flaked paper-thin slices.
meal also known as ground almonds; nuts are powdered to a fine texture.

BAKING POWDER raising agent consisting mainly of two parts cream of tartar to one part bicarbonate of soda.

BICARBONATE OF SODA also known as baking soda.

BUTTER use either salted or unsalted ("sweet") butter; 125g is equal to 1 stick of butter.

BUTTERMILK sold in the refrigerated section of supermarkets. Made commercially by a method similar to yoghurt.

CARDAMOM native to India; has a distinctive aromatic, sweetly rich flavour and is one of the world's most expensive spices. Purchase in pod, seed or ground form.

CHOCOLATE
choc bits also known as chocolate chips and chocolate morsels. Hold their shape in baking and are ideal for decorating.
dark eating made of cocoa liquor, cocoa butter and sugar.
milk eating primarily for eating.

CINNAMON STICK dried inner bark of the shoots of a cinnamon tree.

CLOVES dried flower buds of a tropical tree. Have a strong scent and taste so should be used minimally.

COCOA POWDER dried, roasted then ground unsweetened cocoa beans.

COCONUT
desiccated unsweetened, concentrated, dried shredded coconut.
shredded thin strips of dried coconut flesh.

CORNFLOUR also known as cornstarch. Can be made from corn or wheat.

CRAISINS dried cranberries.

CREAM
sour a thick, commercially-cultured soured cream.
thickened whipping cream containing a thickener.

CREAM CHEESE also known as Philadelphia or Philly, a soft cow-milk cheese. Sold at supermarkets.

CREAM OF TARTAR the acid ingredient in baking powder; keeps frostings creamy and improves volume when beating egg whites.

DATES from the date palm tree. They have a thick, sticky texture.

EGGS some recipes call for raw or barely cooked eggs; exercise caution if there is a salmonella problem in your area.

FLOUR
plain an all-purpose flour, made from wheat.
rice a very fine flour, made from ground white rice.
self-raising flour sifted with baking powder in the proportion of 1 cup plain flour to 2 teaspoons baking powder.

GLACÉ FRUIT fruit cooked in heavy sugar syrup and then dried.

GOLDEN SYRUP a by-product of refined sugarcane; pure maple syrup or honey can be substituted.

JAM also known as preserve or conserve.

KUMARA the Polynesian name of an orange-fleshed sweet potato that is often confused with yam.

MAPLE SYRUP a thin syrup distilled from the sap of the maple tree.

MASCARPONE a fresh, unripened, thick, triple-cream cheese with a delicately sweet, slightly acidic flavour.

MILK we used full-cream homogenised milk unless otherwise specified.
sweetened condensed milk with more than half of the water content removed and sugar added to the milk that remains.

NUTMEG the dried nut of an evergreen tree; available in ground form or whole.

NUTS
hazelnut also known as filberts; plump, grape-size, rich, sweet nut having a brown inedible skin that is removed by rubbing heated nuts together vigorously in a tea towel.
macadamias a rich and buttery nut; store in the refrigerator because of the high oil content.
pecans golden-brown, rich buttery nut.
pine nuts also known as pignoli; not, in fact, a nut, but a small, cream-coloured kernel from pine cones.
pistachio pale green, delicately flavoured nut inside a hard off-white shell. To peel, soak shelled nuts in boiling water for 5 minutes; drain, then pat dry with absorbent paper. Rub skins with cloth to peel.

OLIVE OIL made from ripened olives. **Extra virgin** and **virgin** are the first and second press, respectively. **Extra light** or **light** is diluted olive oil, and refers to taste not fat levels.

PASTRY, READY-ROLLED PUFF packaged sheets of frozen puff pastry.

PLAIN SWEET BISCUITS crumbs made from plain, un-iced biscuits or cookies.

POLENTA also known as cornmeal. A flour-like cereal made of dried corn (maize); also the name of the dish made from it.

QUINCE yellow-skinned fruit with hard texture and astringent, tart taste; eaten cooked or as a preserve.

RAISINS dried grapes.

RIND also known as zest. outer layer of citrus fruits.

ROSEWATER extract made from crushed rose petals; available from health food stores and speciality grocers.

SEMOLINA made from durum wheat.

STAR ANISE a dried star-shaped pod whose seeds have an aniseed flavour.

SUGAR
brown a soft, granulated fine sugar containing molasses to give its characteristic colour.
caster also known as finely granulated or superfine table sugar.
demerara small golden-coloured crystal sugar.
icing sugar also known as confectioners' sugar or powdered sugar; granulated sugar crushed with a small amount of cornflour.
pure icing also known as confectioners' sugar, but without the cornflour.
white a coarse, granulated table sugar, also known as crystal sugar.

SULTANAS also known as golden raisins; dried seedless white grapes.

VANILLA EXTRACT obtained from vanilla beans infused in water. A non-alcoholic version of essence.

CONVERSION CHART

MEASURES

One Australian metric measuring cup holds approximately 250ml, one Australian metric tablespoon holds 20ml, one Australian metric teaspoon holds 5ml.

The difference between one country's measuring cups and another's is within a two- or three-teaspoon variance, and will not affect your cooking results. North America, New Zealand and the United Kingdom use a 15ml tablespoon.

All cup and spoon measurements are level. The most accurate way of measuring dry ingredients is to weigh them. When measuring liquids, use a clear glass or plastic jug with the metric markings.

We use large eggs with an average weight of 60g.

DRY MEASURES

METRIC	IMPERIAL
15g	½oz
30g	1oz
60g	2oz
90g	3oz
125g	4oz (¼lb)
155g	5oz
185g	6oz
220g	7oz
250g	8oz (½lb)
280g	9oz
315g	10oz
345g	11oz
375g	12oz (¾lb)
410g	13oz
440g	14oz
470g	15oz
500g	16oz (1lb)
750g	24oz (1½lb)
1kg	32oz (2lb)

LIQUID MEASURES

METRIC	IMPERIAL
30ml	1 fluid oz
60ml	2 fluid oz
100ml	3 fluid oz
125ml	4 fluid oz
150ml	5 fluid oz (¼ pint/1 gill)
190ml	6 fluid oz
250ml	8 fluid oz
300ml	10 fluid oz (½ pint)
500ml	16 fluid oz
600ml	20 fluid oz (1 pint)
1000ml (1 litre)	1¾ pints

LENGTH MEASURES

METRIC	IMPERIAL
3mm	⅛in
6mm	¼in
1cm	½in
2cm	¾in
2.5cm	1in
5cm	2in
6cm	2½in
8cm	3in
10cm	4in
13cm	5in
15cm	6in
18cm	7in
20cm	8in
23cm	9in
25cm	10in
28cm	11in
30cm	12in (1ft)

OVEN TEMPERATURES

These oven temperatures are only a guide for conventional ovens. For fan-forced ovens, check the manufacturer's manual.

	°C (CELSIUS)	°F (FAHRENHEIT)	GAS MARK
Very slow	120	250	½
Slow	150	275-300	1-2
Moderately slow	170	325	3
Moderate	180	350-375	4-5
Moderately hot	200	400	6
Hot	220	425-450	7-8
Very hot	240	475	9

ARE YOU MISSING SOME OF THE WORLD'S FAVOURITE COOKBOOKS?

The Australian Women's Weekly Cookbooks are available from bookshops, cookshops, supermarkets and other stores all over the world. You can also buy direct from the publisher, using the order form below.

TITLE	RRP	QTY	TITLE	RRP	QTY
Asian, Meals in Minutes	£6.99		Great Lamb Cookbook	£6.99	
Babies & Toddlers Good Food	£6.99		Greek Cooking Class	£6.99	
Barbecue Meals In Minutes	£6.99		Healthy Heart Cookbook	£6.99	
Basic Cooking Class	£6.99		Indian Cooking Class	£6.99	
Beginners Cooking Class	£6.99		Japanese Cooking Class	£6.99	
Beginners Simple Meals	£6.99		Kids' Birthday Cakes	£6.99	
Beginners Thai	£6.99		Kids Cooking	£6.99	
Best Food	£6.99		Lean Food	£6.99	
Best Food Desserts	£6.99		Low-carb, Low-fat	£6.99	
Best Food Fast	£6.99		Low-fat Feasts	£6.99	
Best Food Mains	£6.99		Low-fat Food For Life	£6.99	
Cakes, Biscuits & Slices	£6.99		Low-fat Meals in Minutes	£6.99	
Cakes Cooking Class	£6.99		Main Course Salads	£6.99	
Caribbean Cooking	£6.99		Middle Eastern Cooking Class	£6.99	
Casseroles	£6.99		Midweek Meals in Minutes	£6.99	
Chicken	£6.99		Muffins, Scones & Breads	£6.99	
Chicken Meals in Minutes	£6.99		New Casseroles	£6.99	
Chinese Cooking Class	£6.99		New Classics	£6.99	
Christmas Cooking	£6.99		New Finger Food	£6.99	
Chocolate	£6.99		Party Food and Drink	£6.99	
Cocktails	£6.99		Pasta Meals in Minutes	£6.99	
Cooking for Friends	£6.99		Potatoes	£6.99	
Creative Cooking on a Budget	£6.99		Salads: Simple, Fast & Fresh	£6.99	
Detox	£6.99		Saucery	£6.99	
Dinner Beef	£6.99		Sauces, Salsas & Dressings (May '06)	£6.99	
Dinner Lamb	£6.99		Sensational Stir-Fries	£6.99	
Dinner Seafood	£6.99		Short-order Cook	£6.99	
Easy Australian Style	£6.99		Slim	£6.99	
Easy Curry	£6.99		Sweet Old Fashioned Favourites	£6.99	
Easy Spanish-Style	£6.99		Thai Cooking Class	£6.99	
Essential Soup	£6.99		Vegetarian Meals in Minutes	£6.99	
Freezer, Meals from the	£6.99		Vegie Food	£6.99	
French Food, New	£6.99		Weekend Cook	£6.99	
Fresh Food for Babies & Toddlers	£6.99		Wicked Sweet Indulgences	£6.99	
Get Real, Make a Meal	£6.99		Wok, Meals in Minutes	£6.99	
Good Food Fast	£6.99		TOTAL COST:	£	

Mr/Mrs/Ms _____

Address _____

_____ Postcode _____

Day time phone _____ Email* (optional) _____

I enclose my cheque/money order for £ _____

or please charge £ _____

to my: ☐ Access ☐ Mastercard ☐ Visa ☐ Diners Club

PLEASE NOTE: WE DO NOT ACCEPT SWITCH OR ELECTRON CARDS

Card number ☐☐☐☐ ☐☐☐☐ ☐☐☐☐ ☐☐☐☐ ☐☐☐☐

Expiry date _____ 3 digit security code (found on reverse of card) _____

Cardholder's name _____ Signature _____

To order: Mail or fax – photocopy or complete the order form above, and send your credit card details or cheque payable to: Australian Consolidated Press (UK), Moulton Park Business Centre, Red House Road, Moulton Park, Northampton NN3 6AQ, phone (+44) (0) 1604 497531 fax (+44) (0) 1604 497533, e-mail books@acpmedia.co.uk or order online at www.acpuk.com

Non-UK residents: We accept the credit cards listed on the coupon, or cheques, drafts or International Money Orders payable in sterling and drawn on a UK bank. Credit card charges are at the exchange rate current at the time of payment.

Postage and packing UK: Add £1.00 per order plus 50p per book.

Postage and packing overseas: Add £2.00 per order plus £1.00 per book.

All pricing current at time of going to press and subject to change/availability.

Offer ends 31.12.2006

* By including your email address, you consent to receipt of any email regarding this magazine, and other emails which inform you of ACP's other publications, products, services and events, and to promote third party goods and services you may be interested in.